The Whole World Is Out Or Busy

Irwin B. Meisel, CLU

THE NATIONAL UNDERWRITER COMPANY
505 GEST STREET
CINCINNATI, OHIO 45203

First Edition

Second Printing

505 Gest Street
Cincinnati, Ohio 45203

Library of Congress Catalog Number 86-61182
International Standard Book Number 0-87218-048-4

Printed in the United States of America

Dedication

I dedicate this book to my second eldest daughter, Leslie. When we are the second child we sometines feel our parents rank us in that order. As parents we sometimes unwittingly promote this feeling. If anyone doubts me, go to your photo albums and count the pictures you have of your firstborn, and then count those of your second and subsequent offspring. It's natural to have more time to spend with an only child than it is to divide that time equally among a full flock.

In front of the public who will read this book (in large numbers, I hope) I openly and unashamedly scream that the love of Sharon and me is first when it comes to Leslie. Of course, that ranks her only in a four-way tie with our other daughters. However, Leslie is a very special person and our love never has or never will be "out or busy" when it comes to her.

IBM

Contents

List of Illustrations

1

Soft Shell and Soft Sell

The insurance business itself is nothing more than a numbers game. There are only two laws that dictate the entire affair. The marketing people, actuaries, and salespeople like me who have better ideas are necessary to the schematics. Yet from day one only two laws pertain; everything else is a product of fertile brains. I write books and dream up illustrations on how to present the product in a clearer and more clever fashion so the listener's brain circuitry computes faster and more accurately. However, if the two laws did not exist, there would be nothing for any of us so-called professionals to do.

The first law is the law of large numbers; the commonly termed mortality table. Law number two is the law of compound interest. If anyone thinks universal life is a product of the minds of actuaries, they are right. However, if the same person thinks we could have the product without the use of computers, that person is dead wrong. With all the variables possible in that product and others which are interest sensitive, it would take a career to figure out one policy if the computer were not available.

The old ball game is going into extra innings; the outcome of the world series between traditional term and whole life on the one side, and universal and other interest sensitive products on the other is still on the playing field. There may never be a clear-cut winner. However, no matter what the explosion of ideas, inventiveness of the minds of men, and the awesome power of the computer bring, there are still only two laws that determine the fate of this product we know as life insurance. There is only so much juice in the orange and computer expositions of fantastic numbers in favor of one product of the two laws versus another product of the same two laws are only suppositions which will take decades to prove. In the final shakedown, the mortality and large numbers will speak for themselves.

For the moment, let us put product aside and speak of the large numbers that we salespeople are used to; namely, the calls we have to make to get results. When making my phone calls to do my appointed rounds of selling and servicing, I often tell myself that the whole world is out or busy. In an unofficial survey I conducted, I found I only complete thirty percent of my phone calls on the first try. The other seventy percent are in conference, on the phone, out of town, unavailable, must call back, busy, with a client, or other real or imagined "outs or busys." I occasionally amuse myself by asking, "Is Jim out?" instead of "Is Jim in?" I do this so the answer is "Yes." In this way I don't get a "No" and I don't feel rejected. Mind you, it's a backhanded "Yes" but it is a positive and not a negative.

The use of the phone is a tremendous asset in our business considering the urban population is spread all over. It is a tremendous advantage to get ten or twenty "No's" in an hour rather than driving all over suburbia to get one or two. The phone is our ally but at the same time a foe because we all get call reluctance from time to time and are afraid to pick up the black monster. Maybe that's why the phone companies are now using designer phones and exotic colors. The rebuff is just as great on a Pierre Cardin laser phone as it is on the rotary dial phone but it's classier to use the trendy kind.

The real question is what do we do with our time while using the phone. We must agree the phone is a valuable adjunct to our business. However, the law of averages applies to our business no matter what method one uses to get his or her story on the table in front of the public. The title of the book and this short treatise on the phone doesn't have much to do with the instrument itself. The point is that selling is a business of exposure, just as every other business. That exposure requires a certain number of calls either in person, on the phone, or through the mass media. A certain proportion will be successful and the complementary proportion will be unsuccessful. It has always been so and it will always be.

My daughter, Shelley, entered the life insurance business in early 1984. Under her method of operation, she is closing sales at an average of one out of two. From her first day in the business, I explained the simplicity of making sufficient calls to support herself in exactly the correct ratio desired, considering the effort expended. Having established her closing percentage, I explained that each interview is half a sale. Now when I ask her how an interview went, she tells me she made half a sale. I don't know if it is the selling half or the strike out half. If she closes a big one, it is still half a sale. If she strikes out in grand style, it is still half a sale. In this frame of mind, there is no concentration on looking for the big one. Each face-to-face meeting with a prospective buyer is half a sale. The results for each of us are the same. No matter what your closing percentage is, each interview is a portion of a sale. If it takes four interviews to close one sale, each interview is a fourth of that sale.

The point simply is that this is a selling business and no one is successful all the time. Abraham Lincoln said, "You can fool some of the people some of the time. . .etc." In selling the rule is you can close some of the people some of the time but you can't close all of the people all of the time. It is necessary to make enough calls to satisfy each individual capacity and desire. Some calls will be good and some won't; some will even be bad. Remember, though, that each call will be part of a sale.

Amazing things can happen over the phone and I have even learned to use the languishing time. Part of the calls will result in our being put on "hold." There are a number of things you can do while on hold; the most unproductive of which is to sit and wait and anticipate the instant when your party will be available. Being on hold can take just a few seconds or quite a few minutes. If no one checks back with you, it becomes a matter of courtesy whether or not to hang up and dial over (figuring you have been forgotten) or to dial again later. No matter which you choose, the time spent on hold doing absolutely nothing is a complete waste. Some firms have anticipated the boring or anxious effect holding can have upon people and have installed radio music or news services to keep the caller amused while waiting. This is very considerate and does lend a more caring approach to phone etiquette.

Since it is guaranteed that a part of your telephone time will be spent on hold, it makes sense to find something productive to do during these short intervals. I have discovered three things I can do to make the hold time more welcome and not one of frustration. Years ago I took a hint from my Chinese language study days and from the homework my kids would do. I remember the rote device of learning to utilize flash cards. In the usual form, a question or problem appears on one side of a small, convenient card; on the other side is the answer. The student can then rotate the cards studying as long or short as necessary. He or she can also do it at convenient times or places. One can even do it silently in a crowd and not appear goofy or impolite. It becomes somewhat of a game to go through the pack and see what results can be obtained after successive attempts. Looking back, it was one of the earliest forms of Trivial Pursuit, although a very useful one.

I remember standing in the food line while I was in the Army, thumbing through my Chinese character cards. In the best possible circumstance, the student will have another who is studying the same course and will alternate the asking and answering drills.

Just like my thoughts on the two main laws of the life insurance scheme, there is nothing new on the face of the earth. I have just adapted this style of learning to my life insurance practice. Yet there is only one time and place during which I use this method: while on the phone and while on hold. As soon as I am asked whether or not I want to hold for my party, I make a decision. If I hold, I immediately push the conference button on my phone so my hands are free but enable me to hear any conversation on the other end. I then open my top left-hand desk drawer and take out one of three bundles of flash cards which I have accumulated. In these piles are ideas, sayings, power phrases of mine or someone else's, tax strategies, humorisms, definitions, or other quick, short one-or two-liners.

I flash through the pack for as long as I am on hold. The cards are short and I feel no sense of loss or incompleteness when my party comes on the line. I immediately stop studying and pick up my phone. It is astounding how much studying I get in this way. It brings to the front of my mind many valuable concepts which may have slipped away. It is also surprising how frequently the very conversation in which I am engaged will lead to a point where I can cite some thought I read only a few seconds before. It keeps me sharp in front of my marketplace and adds to the confidence I have in my telephone technique. In addition, this brush up training keeps my mind open to receive new ideas to supplement the old ones.

My card collection grows and grows as the ideas and quips are added. I am constantly dictating material so it can be added to the 3″x5″ cards I use for this flash system. Friends and competitors have even asked to copy my cards to give them a head start when they are beginning their own flash card library.

These cards contain nothing of a deep intellectual nature or anything which requires long hours of memorization. Some of them are only one word long, but the typical card is two or three sentences. I'll cite a few examples:

Automatic Premium Loan—holding pattern.

Cash Value—Owner's account.

Face Value—Beneficiary's account.

Estate Planning is social security for the rich.

"Either I will find a way. . .or I will make one."

. . .Sir Philip Sidney

"What can be done by man can be done by Meisel."

Sensitive Listening.

$300,000 is a lot of money but it doesn't cost a lot to buy the $300,000.

Section 6166—buy now, pay later plan.

The doctor with three patients is seeing one for his staff, one for the government, and one for himself.

For the client who calls up after being disturbed by another agent or having read about a fascinating policy—most times they are no different than the "New and Improved" stuff shown on TV. How many times can you improve your soap or deoderant?

The result of this exercise is that I have put my telephone time to good use even if I'm not talking. Occasionally, the other party will apologize for keeping me on hold for so long or even wonder why I stayed on the line for a relatively lengthy period. I thank him or her for having put me on hold and tell them how happy I was to wait. I explain what I was doing for the thirty seconds or minute or two and they get a little better appreciation for my respect of time and knowledge. This even puts me more in demand as the type of agent with whom they want to do business. Some of them even quiz me on the idea and have adopted it for themselves.

A second way in which I make my hold time worthwhile is to read all about short items that come in the mail and seem unimportant at the time they come. I used to put them all in a folder and promise myself I would get to them later when I had the time. Now I have the time. When I am put on hold I push the conference button and grab the tidbit file. In this file are all those field information bulletins we get from the home offices, flyers from other companies or brokerage services, bank or lawyer or accountant newsletters, advertisements which looked interesting when I first got them, or even letters I want to reread before I dump them. These items are usually not vital so I can start one while on hold and if I don't finish it before I get connected, I don't feel bad. Some of these items are very short or not worth finishing once I get into them so I am able to scrap a lot of paper, but only after having given it a fair chance.

However, my absolute favorite method of equalizing the ball game against "out", "busy", or "hold" is to put the phone on conference mode, close my eyes and meditate. I am able to take about eight or nine one-minute breaks during the course of the day and refresh myself while I am conducting my phone business. After a few years of training myself in relaxing exercises (which take about twenty minutes and are designed to relieve stress) I am able to meditate or rest, almost instantly. This idea also cancels the possibility of the opposite effect which sometimes happens—that of steaming about how much of one's time other people are wasting.

The last three items about maximizing time while combining phone and study or meditation have been very profitable for me. I recommend them to anyone who wants to fight back against the counterproductive influences which hit us every day. The one thing I don't do is just sit and wait; that's the worst possible investment of time.

We have to make the phone calls and we have to make personal calls. We must constantly be exposing ourselves to the high highs of victory and the low lows of defeat. Success can only come if we are exposed to failure. Yet failure can come whether or not there was ever any glimmer of success. Great numbers of potential sales is the only way an agent can succeed. With this constant search for success comes the constant threat of misses. And with this vast display of the law of large numbers comes the nether world of delay and postponements. Thankfully, the more "outs" or busy's" we hear, the more yes's we hear. But we must continue to make the calls. No matter how many times we strike out, we must persist in making new attempts or we will not be busy; in this business, we may be elsewhere.

We work by appointment only but we could say we work by disappointment only. We have to filter through a ton of raw product to net one sale. The raw product is the large list of prospects we must maintain in order to find those who qualify for the right to be clients. Factually, the right word is disappointment. We face enough rejection in one week to last a lifetime in other industries. My point is that the wrong word is discouragement. An agent must understand that the process he or she faces is exactly the one which is faced by an athlete, scientist, inventor, gold panner, or any other person who is engaged in the business of living by his or her own efforts. When the whole world is out or busy, we may have a right to be disappointed. But there is no reason to be discouraged if one will let the law of averages work for him or her.

I was fortunate during my early career to have had the late A.G. Billesdon as my manager. He was a disciple of doing a great number of interviews. Two of his biggest virtues were that of being a true manager, and being accessible. From the time he entered the managerial ranks, he gave up his career of writing insurance. He dedicated his full efforts to helping young agents succeed. With this in mind, he was on the scene daily at regular hours. He did not compete with his agents either for time or prospects. When a young person had a problem, he or she was not faced with the manager being out of town or out on his own personal interviews.

If there was trouble in the life of the rookie, or even veteran agent, it was solved the very day it surfaced because Mr. Billesdon could spot it immediately and deal with it posthaste. There was no reason a financial or emotional problem lingered around the office. If a kid had a problem paying the phone bill and if he was worth keeping, Mr. Billesdon would find a way of having that financial crisis erased that very day. His philosophy was to have agents worry about getting appointments and not about the destructive concerns which were small in the big picture. Some managers recruit and retain as if they are getting a bounty for each agent hanging around the office, but not Mr. Billesdon. The goal was to help the young agent and not further the self-enlightened interests of the manager.

His assessment of the managerial purpose dictated that if an agent failed, it was not the fault of the agent. Rather, it was the fault of the manager either because of bad training or bad selection. Mr. Billesdon was convinced the problem was never one of poor training so when an agent left the business, it was because of faulty selection. He would scrutinize his own fact finding regarding an agent's past and the future potential. But even a man who was as meticulous in his screening efforts as was Mr. Billesdon, had his strikeouts. The law of large numbers takes it's toll even with those who carefully screen the potential for error. Like all of us, he had to rely on more and more sample exposures to make the selling of the career work for him.

His error margin was slight but he also had his ratio of good efforts to bad efforts. He knew the law of large numbers worked in all aspects of life because all areas of life are selling. Everyone is a salesperson; we are all selling goods or services. The hourly employee sells his or her skills on a per hour basis. The doctor sells his or her knowledge on a per visit or per surgery basis. The direct sales agent sells his or her product on a per sale basis. Ergo, the calls have to be made. It was interesting to see how Mr. Billesdon tied in his traits of accessibility with the law of averages.

Salespeople like to congregate; coffee is popular, meetings are popular, but the most popular has to be the bull session. In the early days these clubhouse meetings were held in, what was referred to as, the "bullpen." Today, with fancy room dividers and cubicles, it is tough for the wordy agent to find a forum although I am sure the inventive ones in each office are still holding court. This time spent together can either be productive, if the conversation is of the positive, instructive nature, or it can be worthless, if it consists of a rehash of the morning newscast and the sports scores.

We have all heard of the open-door policy but some profess it merely in words but not in fact. Mr. Billesdon kept his door open ninety-eight percent of the time. When it was closed, there was something really serious going on. If an agent was not in his office, the home office had some weighty news, so he closed the door. If an agent was in there, shame on him.

With the open-door policy came the invitation to have the bull sessions right there with Mr. Billesdon sitting in. He arrived at half past seven and usually had the tedious chores done by nine o'clock. Then he was ready for the agents as they started to arrive. By his actions, he invited their participation each morning in an impromptu meeting. He let the conversation drift to the idle pratter. Slyly, he would ask, "Meisel, how did you do last night?" He would always pick out the one whom he knew had made a sale so the conversation would start off on a winning note. Generally, it would stay on this positive wave for quite a while. When it slipped into the negative or when it got back to sports and the opposite sex, he ended it all with a question which embodied it to the last layer of the law of large numbers. He would wait until someone mentioned something which had nothing to do with business and then dryly ask, "What does that have to do with getting interviews?" It was his way of saying the meeting was over and, at the same time, conveying what our whole career was about. As soon as he said it, everyone knew it was time to make their appointed rounds. If the conclave did not break up fast enough he would wait until someone else spoke and, no matter what was said, he would ask, "Kaufman, what does that have to do with getting interviews?" He never had to say it more than twice.

Mr. Billesdon rarely called a meeting. When new products came out or there was something that had to be published, he just announced it at the impromptu meetings that occured in his office. He got the message across but never made it appear that attendance was mandatory. However, when it was necessary, he got everyone back to the reality of what the whole job was about; the numbers game of making calls.

Making calls, when compared to the retail business, just means your store is open. If you don't make the calls you aren't advertising. How will the new customers know you are trying to reach them if they don't hear from you? Even after 28 years in business there is no way I can make a living if I don't make the calls. The black monster doesn't ring with sufficient business to pay its own way. Times change and it's hard to find a black phone anywhere today but the relationship of calls to success is still the same; that law has not been modified at all.

Yet there is one immutable law of getting someone to return a call to you; just leave your office. The instant you are out of communication the big prospect whom you have been trying to contact returns the call. This is an amazing phenomenon but it does happen in just that fashion. I'm always astounded by how frequently it happens such that I leave the office precisely two minutes before the time recorded on the telephone message I get when I return. I quickly try to reach my party, thinking I now have an interested listener, but I find myself in the "out or busy" syndrome once again.

Another annoyance of the same type is the phone message which is handed to you saying your key prospect called while you were on the phone. You steam a little bit and try to get him or her right back but now it's the prospect's turn to be "out or busy."

It ain't easy being an insurance agent. The negatives are sure there if we want to look for them, but our job is to know the odds and stay with the panning long enough to find the gold. All the humorous but hard things I have mentioned about our profession are controllable. We know the odds will work out precisely over the long haul. Our main job is to give them the chance to work in our favor just by doing the dialing enough times.

Let your fingers do the walking enough times and you will find yourself running to the bank more often.

Merlin Terrill, CLU, in his MDRT address of June, 1984, recited a poem of anonymous authorship which summarizes this introductory chapter:

Make Calls

He is nothing, he can do nothing, he can achieve
  nothing, without making calls.
If you are poor, make calls,
If you are rich, continue making calls.
If you are burdened with seemingly unfair
  responsibilities, make calls.
If you are happy, keep right on making calls.
Idleness gives room for doubts and fear.
If disappointments come, make calls.
If your health is threatened, make calls.
Make calls as if your life were in peril. It really is.
No matter what ails you, make calls.
Making calls is the greatest remedy available for
  both mental and physical affliction.

I agree fully with the poem and I add the following: Make calls even if at times it seems "The Whole World Is Out Or Busy."

2

Selling is Competing

Feel the Laces

Football is a game that has many of the attributes and hazards as our business of selling. Not only does it have the same competitive nature and same compulsion to be successful, but it also places the same high priority on the necessity for careful, continuous preparation. In football points are scored and games are won on the playing field. In insurance points are scored and sales are made in front of the prospective buyers. But in both endeavors, paper plays a gigantic role in getting ready for the drama. Both businesses require playbooks that never stop growing. In football the rules and defenses change all the time; therefore, the need for updating the playbook is constant. In insurance, the laws and rates change all the time; therefore, the need for updating the ratebook and the playbook is also constant.

Football requires a game plan for each encounter; so does selling. Football has become one of the world's greatest critic's sports because of the tremendous TV coverage, marvelous commentators, video replay machines, and other gadgets of the twentieth century. Our sport isn't too much different considering the tape recorders, video recorders, seminars, meetings, and other gadgets of the twentieth century. Football has fewer encounters per season than has the insurance sales profession. As a result, football players have a longer preparation time between games. We in the sales arena don't have the luxury of as much time between appointments in which we could concentrate all our efforts on the upcoming joust. This is not to say that we should not put more effort into getting ready for each interview; however, there may not be enough time to see all the game films and check the height, weight, and past performance of our prospects.

Many interviews fall into the area of just plain scrimmages because we do routine patterns and wait for the variants to make themselves known.

Other interviews are larger or more important and for these we spend more time getting ourselves in the best possible selling situation. This includes doing all the research necessary for that particular case, whether it is better qualifying with a referror, more reviewing of the file, a brushup on the laws, Dun and Bradstreet reports, or other knowledge which can be garnered.

I never played major league football but I was on some teams where we had coaches whose job it was to get us into the best possible playing environment. One of these was a man who had adopted a philosophy which he had heard from another coach and who then brought it to us. In insurance, as in football, it ain't good to fumble. Our coach's idea was to cut down on the fumbling by making the ball a part of the anatomy of those who handled it. Accordingly, he issued a football to those players, namely, the backs. The instructions were to carry the ball with them everywhere they went for two days before the game. This included class, home, transportation (public or private), movies, concerts, and so forth.

The object was to make the ball seem so much a part of the player's movements that it appeared to be a part of his body. Sometimes, it was tough to juggle that thing with school books or to find a place for it at the dinner table so it wouldn't roll too far and knock over the ketchup bottle. We would walk down streets and toss the thing from hand to hand. We would watch television and roll the ball from one side to the other. At first, it was also embarrassing to explain why we were carrying that thing around to the bathroom or to a semi-final exam. However, after a while, it became so second nature to us that any questions were the disturbance and not the job of lugging around the pigskin.

The players became used to the feel of the grain of the ball. They learned to sense where it was tapered and where it was fat. They got to know that it was divided into quadrants. They could sense the difference between one with too much air or too little. They soon realized the distance between the two points on the ends. And they felt the laces which was the focal point of the ball. The ball became a completely natural part of them.

It worked!! The fumbles were cut down dramatically.

The obvious question is, "What has this got to do with insurance? There are no laces on a policy." Just the opposite, I contend there is the same kind of handle on a case as there is with the laces on a football. I try to do all the digging that is necessary to get ready for a case in sufficient time so I can have the completed file in my hands at least one day before the appointment (and, if possible, two or three days.) This means all of the legal supplementary work, if any, any proposals or documentation, any correspondence from insurance companies or other sources and, most importantly, the simplified proposal.

Other things have happened to the file before it gets into my hands. I will have started the work by making the initial contact and dictating a note or notes to the secretaries who will start pulling the various components together. To that end, I try to give them enough time to do their work so there is no strain as the interview time arrives. Most of my material is on computer or in simplified proposal form which takes time to simmer down from the fattened piles of paper where we begin the individualized work for each specific case.

Another analogy I have stolen from football is the two minute warning. This alerts the opposing teams that only this short time remains in a game so final plans can be formulated. In our office it is known as the Two Minute Drill. There are more mistakes going on in the insurance business today than I have ever seen in nearly three decades. I don't fully understand the reasons but the fact of the matter is that the information explosion has caused a service gap. We all make our mistakes but the time I take to correct or expunge them probably accounts for forty percent of my working hours. This includes my own, my staff's, the clients', but most ominously the home offices.' To head off the dire consequenses of furthering or compounding the errors, I have instituted the game plan of the Two Minute Drill.

Under the Two Minute Drill system, I ask each staff member to take an extra two minutes after each task is finished just to turn the pages or give a once-over look to the file. This is so they can be proud of themselves in having done a part of the case preparation upon which others will build. On the other hand, it is to help them spot an obvious mistake that would have hampered the whole process or caused embarassment later in front of our clients. It is amazing how many little, stupid typos, forgotten or botched items show up if one will just take these two minutes to look at his or her work and let the brain circuitry run through the cycle one time.

Now, having gone through the Two Minute Drill, we borrow from the refreshment phase of the sports world. It is known as the Sandwich. I am not speaking of food but the idea of putting the right ingredients into the right place. After, or even during, the period when the various parties are putting a file together, I will make up the order of appearance of the different elements of a case. On the preliminary draft of the agenda, I will make notes of what is still outstanding and who is doing it. As the items are completed, they are put in the file in the order listed on the agenda. This is known as the Sandwich. I am not kidding about this; in my office we refer to this first brief of a case as the Sandwich. After one complete Sandwich is made and checked, we construct as many copies as we need, but they all refer back to and duplicate the Sandwich.

When all of the work that is necessary for a case is finished, it comes to me in a complete Sandwich. Hopefully, this is two days before the interview; at the latest it should be one day. Only under the most extreme situations would I want to grab a file from someone else and go into a meeting. When I get the file, I allow myself the time to sit down with it and "feel the laces." I already know what it contains since I have been in on the process of getting the agenda ready, but I now have it in the final form. Just like the days when I used to fondle the football, I hold the file, leaf through it, or study it intensely, if needed. Sometimes, if it's a case which is complicated or diverse, I will take the file home the night before the interview. Truthfully, I may not even open it but the mere fact of having it available allows for some sense of vibrations of what is in it.

On the other hand, I may spend some intense time laboriously going over the presentation one more time, or it may be as simple as doing the Two Minute Drill. In any event, it is a matter of advance preparation. I can sincerely state that most of my sales are made in my office during the preparation phase. The interview itself is just a matter of acting out the visualization of what went on in the process of getting ready. I feel comfortable and loose knowing I have the file with me so I can refer to it at will. If changes are needed, I still have time to get them done before I have to make the presentation. There is also a feeling of complete familiarity with the items in the file, therefore, the interviews go smoother. For me, the whole process leads to more completions and fewer fumbles.

In the age of high-tech, high-touch and, therefore, high-tension, I say relax, make it easy, do the Two Minute Drill, make a Sandwich, and feel the laces.

The Broken Play

Sometimes, in spite of all the hype, and in spite of what President Harry Truman said, we all let the buggers get us down. It would be unnatural to be "up" all the time. If you were, there would be no way to know when you were up or when you were down. There has to be some basis for comparison. We all try as hard as we are able to keep our attitudes positive and our selling circumstances free of hindrances. But on occasion, a bad mood can creep in and we can find ourselves in the depths of a foul depression. Sometimes it is possible to be in this mood and not even be aware of it ourselves. It just happens; it's normal and nothing over which to hire a new shrink.

When this glum atmosphere hits, our staff and associates may ask us, "Is everything OK?" If this happens, it may be time to examine our positive signs for a face doesn't lie too often. There are other times when we ourselves can sense a lower attitude level. If you can talk yourself out of one of these moods, you're lucky. If not it's probably best to stay away from the public for a little while and try to get yourself unwound from the tenseness.

Selling is one of the world's most inexact sciences and what applies usually does not apply regularly. For every truism we learn and practice, there is a situation where the opposite formula is the winner. One of the funniest "no-brain" selling experiences I can recall was a situation that should never have turned out as it did. I still can't explain it except to say, "Even a blind squirrel finds a chestnut once in a while."

The law of averages applies to everything in life and every so often, if you make enough calls, you will eventually find someone who wants precisely what you have and no amount of stupidity can dissuade him/her from having it. This happens in sports when a play goes awry and the crowd expects the worst. Yet through sheer luck and automatic reactions by the offense, a large, fortuitous gain or score is earned. The sports media guys call it the Broken Play. I guess we all have them from time to time. On occasion, we may even convince ourselves that we had the situation under control, although we know it was sheer blind luck that saved the loss. The story I will now relate fits the mold of the announcers' stereotype so closely that I will use their description. This is truly a Broken Play.

Grant, a young agent, asked me for joint assistance in calling on a corporate prospect, an area in which Grant was not familiar. The corporation was a large Detroit employer and had 4000 employees. We made an approach on a "checklist" basis and found some interest in the areas of deferred compensation and cafeteria plans. I indicated that we would arrange another appointment when we could come back with the expert, Jerry, in the field of administration.

On the day before the appointment, I received a phone call from Bill, an associate of Jerry's, who said that Jerry had to go out of town and would not be able to keep the appointment which we had set up. Bill said that he had the entire presentation on a slide carousel and could do the same interview that I had seen Jerry do in the past. I had no choice but to say that it was alright. He mentioned that their slide projection was not available and asked if I had one. I told him we did.

On the day of the appointment, we were to meet at my office at 8:30am and then drive together to the office of the client for the 9:00am call. Grant arrived at 8:25 and I asked him for the file so I could spend just five minutes quickly reviewing the little bit of data we had; Bill had the other material that we needed for the day. Grant looked embarrassed and I knew immediately that he had left the file elsewhere. I started to get bad feelings about the way things were shaping up but we were still in a "Go" pattern. At 8:35am Bill called to verify that I had the slide projector. I told him that he was already five minutes late and to please hurry. His office was only a few minutes away and he arrived at mine at 8:45. I knew then that we were going to be late and I began to get into an angry, foul mood. If I were the only agent on the case, I would have postponed the meeting, but since there were the two of them and they did not seem too perplexed, I decided to carry on. They could tell by my near silence that I was not as happy as I should have been.

In my car, I asked Grant to become familiar with the slide equipment. He was in the back seat and there seemed to be a lot of futile fidgeting going on. When I asked about the problem, he told me he could not get the carousel to fit. Bill tried to help him out at which time they both discovered that the carousel was a Kodak and my machine was a Minolta. There was a lot of fumbling going on but the plain fact turned out to be incompatability. I asked Grant to insert one of the slides by hand and it fit. I told him he would have to put them in one at a time like they used to do in the olden days. My patience level was gone and I figured we had blown everything so far and the case would be lost.

As I had figured, we arrived fifteen minutes late. When we pulled up to the guardhouse we noticed the vice-president we were going to see in the car ahead of us. His parking spot was alongside the guardhouse and as he got out of his car, he saw us going through the gate to the visitor's lot. He seemed very jovial as he waved enthusiastically. After we were inside the lobby and signed the register, the young lady he had sent to meet us took us to his office. I was still in glum spirits, thinking we should have made a phone call with an excuse to call off the meeting. Our prospect greeted us warmly and asked that we step down to the conference room. When we got there we met one of the other vice-presidents and a secretary, Lori, who was going to sit in on the meeting and take notes.

I thought everything had gone wrong so far and I felt we were not conducting the appointment under the favorable circumstances which I would have liked. So, in attempting to get it all back into the right synchronization, I called the meeting to order by saying, "Let me kick off the meeting with a short review of what we discussed last time and what we are going to accomplish today." I didn't want anything else to fall apart, if I could help it. The first vice-president said that was a good idea. I really felt he was trying to be forceful with his two other associates and appear knowledgable in a field which was new to him. I truthfully explained our plight and mix-up about the slide equipment, whereupon the vice-president said, "We must have about five of those things around here. We used them in some of our stores, for displays."

He reached under the conference table and picked up the fancy telephone device they had and called someone to ask that they bring the right kind of projector to the room. I think he was really enjoying playing boss, so I let him. The machine arrived and the messenger left. Grant tried to get it to work but was unfamiliar with it. Our client was getting into the helpful mood so he picked up the phone again and asked for another worker. He explained that this man knew all about audio-visual equipment. Again, someone came and set up their machine with our slides and then left. Bill made a very good, concise interview following the outline on the slides. It was brief but effective. They all had a lot of questions which we handled.

The top man said this was the perfect product for them at this perfect time. He explained that they were just about to go into negotiations with their biggest union and had an eye on settling within three months. I asked how many unions they had and he told me they negotiated with thirty-eight locals and this product was something that could be offered and would benefit both the company and the employees equally. He was ecstatic with the product and his enthusiasm made his two cohorts bubbly. He asked what we needed to get a survey going. We told him we could have a report within two weeks if we could get a rapid return of the census information and employer costs of certain items which would qualify for cafeteria compensation. He instructed Lori to make this a priority item and to work with us or our people completely with the goal of getting it all done without any delays or hitches.

By now my bad mood had passed. The attitude was upbeat all the way. When we returned to the car, I told Bill and Grant that this experience only proved the law of averages. See enough people and the results will follow, irrespective of what is said or what is done. In this case we happened to run into the right client with the right product at the right moment. This even surpassed the bumbling of the case preparation and the stupid mood of one of the principal players.

We enter almost a hundred percent of our interviews with the goal of a successful result. We must admit that due to circumstances beyond our control most of these interviews do not result in sales. In fact, nearly all deals look good on paper but, in reality, most of them do not work out. This is a fact of business. Sometimes, in order to get a positive response, it is best to assume a negative result. A good thing can occur by not anticipating too much from every case; in fact, by anticipating some small defeats, you can minimize the heavy impact of rejection. This attitude can instill an atmosphere of complete objectivity and eliminate the area of subjectivity. This neutral ground can convey the message of being in the best interest of the prospect and can pave the way for an unfettered decision from him or her. Please made careful note of the fact that I did not say to have a negative attitude; however, on occasion, assume a negative result. That was my feeling in this case and the result astounded me.

In this book I had no intention of repeating illustrations or theories I had proposed in my other books. Yet, in going around the country on speaking engagements, I have found certain interviews are exceedingly popular with the audiences. One of the most requested is my "Retail-Wholesale" interview (Illustration 2-1.) I present it here not only because some of you have not seen it in previous books, but because of the surprise result in one case which exemplifies simplifying simplicity.

You Don't Understand, Coach

The "Retail-Wholesale" interview has proven to be a fantastic one page opening interview and more often a closing interview. Sometimes I use it on interviews where I'm not quite sure of all the facts of the case. In these events, I think it will be a fact finding interview only but before I realize what's happening, I'm in the middle of a closing interview. Its effect is grabbing upon the listeners. The chart is designed in report form to list all the facts I could think of which were necessary for a buy-sell case. The businessperson can see the major topics on the left and the comparisons of "A-Retail" and "B-Wholesale." Immediately, the mind is preconditioned to like the "Wholesale." As I mentioned earlier, the three words the businessperson knows the best are: 1) Profit; 2) Retail and; 3) Wholesale. In order to make a profit, the businessperson has to buy for a lower price than that which he sells. This price is identified by him and everyone of his suppliers as "Wholesale." The prospect knows before he starts reading that he's going to like the right-hand column the best. My title alone has steered him to what he knows is best. Now it is the job of my explanations to prove he or she has made a wise choice.

For insurance people, there is not too much that needs to be explained about this illustration. Each line itself could be the subject of a long sermon on why the "B" column is better. Probably most of us have done interviews on each of these, using the subject as the entire interview.

Take, for example, "Date of Payment." Isn't this the essence of life insurance itself, especially business insurance? Somebody has to pay something, someday. It certainly makes more sense for all the partners or shareholders to pay while they're all around to do it jointly and in a scientific, periodic manner, even in monthly premiums, if necessary.

Line two, "Principal Payments on Stock" is a fantastically enticing point. I often get the question, "How can you buy something and not pay for it?" My standard response is, "I don't know but that's how it works and I'll give you a contract to substantiate it."

Line three, "Interest Payments" goes hand in hand with line two. If you buy something you have to pay for it—that's principal. If you buy it in installments, the cost includes interest. This is so either under "Retail" where the items are really being paid for, or under "Wholesale" where one is only paying premiums. Here is where I take the liberty of referring to premiums as interest. I sometimes get the question, "If it is interest,

Illustration 2-1

Methods of Transferring a Business Interest at Death

	A — RETAIL	B — WHOLESALE
Date of Payment:	After Death	Before Death
Principal Payments On Stock:	Yes	No
Interest Payments:	Yes	Yes
Amount of Principal:	Determine after death; subject to negotiations with heirs, survivors, attorneys, IRS and other advisors.	Set in advance by agreement.
Amount of Interest:	Variable; determined after death. Assume very favorable rate-8%.	3.2%
Actual Cost:	Full value of shares plus interest = 100% plus interest.	Full value of interest paid by date of death. No principal payments; never reaches 100%.
Timing of Payments:	Start at date of death.	Start discounted payments now. Stop at date of death.

Payments Carried on Books:	Yes; liability after death for negotiated value of shares.	Yes; as asset before death for exact stated equity value on interest payments. (None)
Stock Encumbered After Death:	Yes	No
Buyer at Death:	Unknown — not specified	Corporation
Estate Obligated to Sell at Death:	No	Yes
Discounted Value of Principal and Interest Available at Date of Death, in One Sum:	No	Yes
Payments Waived at Disability of Shareholder:	No	Yes
"Pegged Value" for Estate Taxes:	No	Yes

A. Installment payments after death either to heirs or bank, cash if available, reserve account, borrow or any buy now and pay later plan.
B. Life insurance and proper business agreement.

is it, therefore, deductible?" My response is, "No! I'm referring to a different kind of interest. It's not deductible because you won't spend anything. This is a substitution for the principal which you would have paid to buy the stock asset. That would not be deductible because nothing is spent. You traded one asset for another; in this case, non-deductible interest for the entire value of the business. It's a small price to pay, but worth it."

The "Amount of Principal" refers to the value of the business interest. As I go through this form with the prospects, I elaborate on the various points to whatever extent is necessary. This item in the "Retail" column looks and is complicated. There are these and other people with whom the surviving shareholder has to work. On the other hand the "Wholesale" column is simple and direct. The form is designed to clearly highlight, not only the clarity but, the superiority of the "Wholesale" method.

The "Amount of Interest" is an area where I can have fun, especially these days with the constant fluctuation in the prime rate. I can be liberal and assume a generous grandparent-type rate of 8%. When I say this, I know most people are disagreeing with me, on the inside. They are saying to themselves that it's a ridiculously low rate and they would never accept it. This shows up the fallibility of the "Retail" way. Then I make it very appetizing with a more ridiculous rate of 3.2%. Right here, I often get the question, "You mean to say we don't have to pay the principle and we still get a low wholesale rate like that? How can you do it?" My response, "I don't know, but I'll give you a contract to prove it." You will readily recognize the 3.2% as the premium of $32 per thousand. If it's a multiple life case, this is the average premium per thousand, with all the lives to be included. If I suspect bad health, I may increase the premium to 3.6% or 4%. When the policy is issued, and if I am close, it's an easy matter to deliver a rated policy. If I overshot the estimate, I'm a hero when I come in with a lower rate.

Sometimes, I don't have to use any other displays other than what you see here. The only thing that ever varies is the "Wholesale" amount of interest. We have this illustration on our word processor. I can get ready for any interview by just looking up the premium, translating that to a percentage, and telling the operator to let me have a "Retail-Wholesale" at 3.2% or whatever. In seconds I have as many freshly typed copies as I need. Thinking of the form took years to develop by meshing all my thoughts on buy-sell insurance. But now I can get ready for the biggest or smallest case in a matter of minutes.

The "Actual Cost" describes the entire cost. Under "Retail" it's the full price that must be paid, plus any finance charges. Under the "Wholesale" it's the premiums. The fact that "Wholesale" never reaches 100% can not be explained any clearer.

Under "Timing of Payments" I explain the "Retail" is an unequal proposition. There is no way of knowing who will pay what, or when; it's bound to be an unequal situation. The survivors will do more work to keep less and the heirs could be shortchanged. Under "Wholesale" it's absolutely equal; the premiums are a known scientific, mathematical function paid by the labors of all partners or shareholders by their earnings from the business, which is in direct proportion to the shares or percentages. Not only are the premium payments equal, but so are the insurance proceeds when they are traded for a business interest at death. A real dollar buys a dollar's worth of the business.

I frequently add, at this point, that under the present setup, with no umpire, I'd want to be the first to die. At least my family would stand a ghost of a chance of collecting something if only because of the novelty of the first death, and the goodwill intention to fulfill the expressed good intentions. The sorrow and grief wears off after a while yet the economic realities start settling in and hedging may start.

The "Payments Carried on Books" section is designed to show the difference between what is owed and what is owned. Under "Retail" if there is a debt after death it obviously has to be booked until it is paid off. Under "Wholesale" the asset value referred to is the cash value of the insurance.

"Stock Encumbered After Death" shows the problem of dealing with bankers, creditors, suppliers, or anyone else who examines the books, gets a Dunn & Bradstreet report, or the company statement. The stock of the company, or even the stock which is being repurchased, has restraints on it. Under "Retail" there is that problem; under "Wholesale" there is none. The encumbrances are gone, paid, obviated.

The "Buyer at Death" is simple to explain but, once again, I have some fun exploring and exhausting the possibilities. Under "Wholesale" it's clear-cut.

In the "Estate Obligated to Sell at Death" section, consider the problem which could exist if the surviving spouse doesn't want to sell. Maybe he or she has a private income and would just like to keep a stock ownership position for equity only. This not only encumbers the business but can immediately create an adversary situation. The cleanest cut is that one party owns the business and the other owns the cash. "Retail" can't do this, "Wholesale" can.

"Discounted Value of Principal and Interest Available at Date of Death, in One Sum" refers to the fact that either the complete package can be finished in one transaction or it can't. This means principal and interest, everything. The two answers speak for themselves.

The subject of "Payments Waived at Disability of Shareholder" is frosting on the cake since it is not a part of "Retail" but an important part of "Wholesale"; namely, waiver of premium. I explain that a shareholder can become disabled, remain so for many years, and then die. The waiver of premium rider can make sure that the deal is completed even under this situation. However, waiver of premium is not a part of the "Retail" basis.

"Pegged Value for Estate Taxes" is especially important in the larger estates and businesses. I explain that a public corporation has a value that can be traded every day on the stock market. But closely held stock only has a real value when someone wants it. For estate tax purposes, though, the IRS says it has a value and they apply the "Doctrine of the Open Till" to determine that value. The tax is computed on the highest basis even if there is not that same intrinsic value to the estate. "Wholesale" solves that problem with a properly drawn document.

The legend at the bottom of the illustration page refers to the letters "A" & "B" at the top. The letters are clear and the words land heavy. The use of this form takes the decision away from insuring or not insuring and places the choice on "A" or "B"; "Retail" or "Wholesale."

There was a humorous interview I conducted in which I used the "Retail-Wholesale" presentation. The setting was a meeting in my office with three principals in a chain of restaurants. I used my overhead projector and did not pass out any information during the meeting to the prospects. When the meeting was over I gave them a hard copy for the business. I conducted the presentation in just the fashion you have studied. After I finished my explanations I attempted to close the sale with the question, "Which way makes more sense, wholesale or retail?"

One of the stockholders was noticeably more excited than the others during the session. He was the first to respond to my question with one of his own. He asked, "How do we go about changing our business to wholesale?" He was so enthused and eager to get the buy-sell agreement and the insurance, he thought he not only had to adopt the ideas I was espousing, but also had to register somewhere with the proper legal or government authorities to change his business format from retail stores to wholesale. I don't know how he would have done that and still served meals to the public, but that was the effect the interview had on him.

I have never had any client as enthusiastic as he was to get going with the program, even to the extent of finding out how to change the entire method of operation. He had missed part of the point of "Methods of Transferring a Business Interest *at Death*." He thought he had to be a wholesale operation, right now.

I took the question as a compliment and, frankly, was pleased with myself at the result this simple format interview had engendered. Selling is competitive but regardless of all the similarities it has with football or other sports, it is not brute strength which prevails but brute perseverance and, sometimes, a little brain power.

3

Syndromes

Business operates in strange and wondrous ways. The personality of a hundred businesses can be as varied as the personality of the hundred business owners. In a small corporation, where the ownership is closer to the input and the output, things seem to get done faster and in a more efficient way. The only thing that is missing is the large volume. Decisions are made and plans carried out. There is a minimum of politics, delays, and paperwork. There is neither time nor money to go through all the fancy trappings of boardroom strategy or committee sabotage.

The larger the business the larger the gap between origination of ideas or production and the delivery of the product. The larger the business the more necessity there is for policies and procedures. Most of these procedures are necessary but some are a function of size and accountability or lack thereof. We do some of these things justice by calling them procedures when that is not what they are at all. They exist and prevail but who can explain them? Some things have to go to the Business Retardation Department before they are ready for consideration. Every company has a Business Retardation Department. In every firm there is at least one place where things get out of sync. The workers in that department don't know their section is called that and, in reality, that is not the name. But in operation, that is what happens in certain segments of every large American company. I have noticed it especially in the head offices of some of the large insurance companies with whom I work.

In business, as in life itself, there are patterns which reoccur. Possibly, they could be called syndromes, or maybe they are just patterns that happen over and over again; maybe that's just the way it is. A syndrome is a pattern that appears to occur over and over again so that is what I call these tongue in cheek little foibles that I have noticed in business. It is surprising how some things seem to gravitate toward one inevitable conclusion or mode of operation.

The following stories are not meant to hurt anyone and are only pointed out in jest. I am sure that to another person's way of thinking, the manner in which I conduct myself falls into a syndrome, but I leave it to them to write their own treatise.

The 41 Memo Syndrome

This section could have been called the number syndrome since I will be considering two phenomena that have to do with numbers. The first will be a reference to the creation of energy; the second will have to do with the destruction of energy.

It is a fact that water will boil at 212 degrees Fahrenheit. At 211 degrees it is very hot. It will burn you and scald you. It will do amazing cooking and cleaning functions, but it will not boil. It boils at 212 degrees and not one smidgen other than that. When it boils, it does an amazing thing: it creates steam and steam is energy.

That energy can be harnessed to do work for mankind. It can move a multi-ton ship, and it can activate generators and turbines which, in turn, perform fantastic functions. The 212th degree is no different than any of the others; it is exactly the same as degree number 1 or degree number 211. But this little bugger piled on top of all the others which accumulate to 212 can provide magic limited only by the parameters of people's brainpower.

In a large corporation the countervaling force equal to the theory of the 212 degrees is the philosophy of 41 Memos. In the operation of The 41 Memo Syndrome, nothing happens until the 41st piece of paper hits the ozone. When it does the action parallels the fury of the 212th degree. Just like the degree hierarchy, the 41st memo is no different than the first memo, except that the flavor changes. Memo 41 may say the same thing as any one of the others but, by this time, it has undergone a number of changes.

One of those changes, which could be the most important, is the fact that the memo has been reworked so the proper author of a good idea is now the ranking official at the home office. Another change is that it has been worked and reworked so the official line of the head office is now a part of the subject. An additional reason for the delay mechanism is the danger of making a decision that is too hasty. Whatever the reason, it takes a while for a good memo to get its proper respect. Certain research must be done and, in certain instances, a sensible period of seasoning must go on. By memo 41, all of these reactions have a chance to come into play and the final posture can be assumed.

Sometimes it is not a matter of authorship but just a matter of the passage of time. Someone will look at the file or the person on the receiving end will start a follow-up campaign and all parties will agree that enough time has elapsed so a decision is nigh and the matter will be settled. It seems the proper period of time for this is about thirteen to fourteen weeks. The exact amount of time is unimportant but it is eerie that all of these things happen with memo 41.

I'll give you an example of how The 41 Memo Syndrome works. On numerous occasions, my office questioned the delay in getting certain cases approved in underwriting. We would receive interim memos from the home office letting us know the status of certain requirements such as EKG's, X-rays, etc. We would often notice that certain things which we had sent were listed as "outstanding." After two such reports to the agency, which were forwarded to us, and two memos to the agency who wrote two computer messages to the underwriter, we received the following message:

SUBJECT: MAX CLIENT
RE: EKG. WHEN THEY COME IN, THEY ARE SEPARATED FROM THE APPLICATION AND SENT TO MEDICAL DEPARTMENT FOR INTERPRETATION. THEY ARE THEN SENT TO PENDING WHEEL TO WAIT FOR APP FILE. APP FILE DOESN'T HIT PENDING WHEEL UNTIL AFTER AN INITIAL REVIEW. ON MY INITIAL REVIEW, I SET UP ALL REQUIREMENTS. USUALLY EKG IS IN PENDING WHEEL AND COMES RIGHT BACK TO ME AND IS CLEARED OFF SYSTEM IN A DAY OR TWO. HOPE THIS HELPS YOU TO UNDERSTAND PROCESS AND ALLEVIATE INITIAL CONCERN. IF EKG STILL SHOWS OUTSTANDING AFTER A WEEK, THEN LET ME KNOW BUT OTHERWISE THERE PROBABLY ISN'T ANY PROBLEM AT ALL. SIGNED, UNDERWRITER.

This memo did clear up a lot of confusion on our part but, more importantly, it helped the agency underwriting person understand for the first time how a set of application papers were handled. It also helped the underwriter realize, for the first time, there was something called a "Pending Wheel." The agency underwriting person was in his position for four years and was in the insurance business for thirty years overall and didn't know that his company had such a system. Up to this point, he would write memos or call whenever a broker would request information on a file which was slow. If we did the tracking, there is no doubt in my mind that we would find he and the home office had written exactly forty memos before that last dandy came in. It is amazing to me that both sides of the process had operated for any length of time without knowing the procedure of the other. I thought it was a goofy memo but it did answer the question of the underwriter.

I make very few underwriter jokes but in the past, and only in jest, I have referred to the underwriting department as the "dartboard." Now, I know my suspicions were correct when the underwriter let us in on the secret of the "Pending Wheel" as a cog in The 41 Memo Syndrome.

The Animal Kingdom Syndrome

We've all heard the phrase, "It's a jungle out there." It refers to the tough conditions of earning our daily bread. It is tough out on the street and making a living in not an easy thing to do. Just staying apace is a chore. It may be a slander to refer to the style of our lives by comparing it to the wild animal kingdom. I assume wild animals have stress, too, and I have no idea what they do to relieve themselves of the fatigue and burnout. Yet I would have no quarrel with them if, in their own private communication, they would say, "It's civilized out there." A pig, or a cow, or a horse, or a lion are all mammals and have the same parts that we as humans do. The only thing we have that they do not is intelligence. They make up for it with such an innate sense of instinct that, if left to their own natural devices, puts us to shame in many of our thought processed activities.

Out there, in that jungle, it is "kill or be killed." That's the way it works for both the wild ones and the civilized ones. The wild ones eat or get eaten. We don't have too much cannibalism but we, in a more subtle fashion, operate on the very identical principle. We first make a stop at the supermarket because we all have to eat when our stomachs get empty. The difference is this thing we call the mind.

In the big picture, the mind is the thing that separates the beasts from the people. However, also in the big picture, if we want to do something right, it is best to look to Mother Nature for guidance. When we walk our dogs down to the corner, or wherever "Doggie Heaven" is in your neighborhood, an interesting thing takes place. Your dog may not only be housebroken but it may never have seen another dog except on television. When you get the dog down to the corner, nature takes over. All that sniffing, scratching, and excitement must have a purpose. Can their sense of smell really be that acute? And what are they smelling that allows the smallest puppy to pull the owner who is on the other end of the leash? We must ponder: who is walking whom?

I have a theory. Mind you, I have not done any research and I don't know the first thing about animals. Yet, I like my theory because it seems to make sense and all the pieces fit together. The only thing these animals have in common when they make that trek is the fact that they are all relieving themselves. That sure makes for a distinctive odor. That has to be their way of communicating with each other when they are not together. After all, they can't write. I have seen the animal shows on TV and heard the explanation that the pattern of urination lays out the territory of some of the clans, families, or prides. The intruder can tell by the scent where one plot begins and another one ends. It seems to work pretty well because, as the shows point out, the hunt only goes on when the animals are hungry. Otherwise, they aren't perturbed by outsiders and there isn't too much squabbling just for the sake of fighting.

In business the same philosophy holds true. There are certain people or whole departments who keep their territories so cluttered with work in-process or so messed up that on a day off no one dares go near their desks. We sometimes see people at their work stations who have titles or job descriptions but we wonder what they do. The work piles warn us that this is forbidden territory and we best stay away. The work itself seems without purpose and only they know what is going on. What is happening here is a little bit of jungle theory. In effect, they are urinating on the desks so that signals go out indicating this is private turf and visitors are not welcome. In this way, they create a little job security. I suppose some of them are obsolete or nonessential but who really knows? When the lions are not hungry they just lay out their territory and take a snooze inside of it. I suspect that is also what is going on behind many desks.

The Second Lieutenant Syndrome

It is humerous how some of these syndromes connect and can be seen in tandem. I guess that falls into the category of, "That's the way it's always been done around here." For example, the first two I mentioned, the 41 Memo Syndrome and the Animal Kingdom, seem to go hand in hand. One of the ways of establishing one's own territory is to write a lot of confusing memos. Probably all of the phenomena that I will speak of will be interchangeable and compatible with one or more of the others.

One of the particularly funny ones is the one that I call the Second Lieutenant Syndrome. When I was in the military service, the person who had the lowest image was not the buck private but the designee know as Second Lieutenant. In the days of the Korean War we had a lot of lieutenants who were either recent ROTC (Reserve Officers' Training Corps.) graduates or who had just completed ninety days of training. They were now the proud possessors of the title, "Officer." In fact, they were also called "90-day Wonders." Usually the "Second Looey" was a short guy who coincided with the period of training that he had just completed.

He was higher in rank than any of the noncommissioned men but usually lower in experience and savvy than most of them. It was always a hilarious scene to see a second lieutenant giving orders to one of the grizzled, veteran master sergeant with twenty-five years of service displayed by hash marks on their sleeves. The master sergeant had to obey the order but he would convey an attitude of, "Who's in charge here?" just by his movement, voice, or silence. He did what he was required to do but he was none too pleasant or prompt about doing it. He knew more about everything than anyone else in the regiment, had served in two wars on ten fronts and understood the big picture. Now he has a shavetail telling him to move whatever was on the right to the left, and whatever was down, up. Most of the time the commands were unimportant but they were the symbol of authority and gave a secure feeling to the boss. There were "make-work" projects that had no bearing on anything except to show the men that the second lieutenant had some game plan. The real thrust was change; more importantly, it was change for change sake. There was no real consequence one way or the other whether or not the job was done.

This method also creeps into business. We have those people who love to give orders and flex their authoritative muscles. They have all their subordinates running around doing tasks just for the sake of doing them.

Then they follow up with the closest of inspections. The whole exercise doesn't amount to a hill of beans but it was the project for the day.

You can easily see that The Second Lieutenant Syndrome could mesh with The 41 Memo or Animal Kingdom ones to make for a deadly duo or trio of Business Retardation activities. Part of the "king of the hill" routine could be to have memos done just to announce the presence of the "boss." For sure, we can see the marriage of The Second Lieutenant with The Animal Kingdom routines. Just look outside your window at the bird feeder and watch the pecking order; any bluejay eats before any sparrow. The sign on the door or the bars on the shoulder make a bluejay out of a sparrow merely by the striping and not by the size or the ability.

Bad diction says, "If it ain't broke, don't fix it." However, that doesn't hold true for the second lieutenant or the first cousin. We see a lot of "bossism" going on with the despots and the nepotists. They are wonderful candidates to proliferate the "change is better" philosophy. Your best bet is to salute when confronted and say to yourself, "He wasn't talking to me; it's the person next to me."

The Consultant Syndrome

Here's a good one. It's called The Consultant Syndrome. In this classic ploy, which is just the opposite of The Animal Kingdom game, one stays clear of the action yet hangs around close enough to get the glory, if available. It is somewhat like The Animal Kingdom, vulture variety.

There are many reasons for the hiring of an outside consultant. It could be that a fresh perspective is needed. It could be that no one within the company really knows the field or subject under consideration. Or it could be any variety of other legitimate reasons. One which is not legitimate, but saves room for credit gathering, is the buffer zone technique of this syndrome. In this category, a high ranking official hires a consulting firm at considerable dollars. If the consultant's report is accepted and it works, our executive takes the credit for hiring the consultant and having the good business sense to foretell what was needed. If the implementations do not work and, in fact, cost a lot of money and wasted time, the consultant is blamed and our executive can shy away from the gambit by blaming the consultant and firing him with the proper fanfare and shame. This way our corporate climber keeps his shiny shoes out of the mess and lives to scheme another day.

All of this is done at great expense to the company. However, the excuse goes that it would have cost ten times as much to have embarked on the program without the consultant's work so, overall, a big savings was earned. I can think of one company with assets in the billions of dollars which went out of business in the United States only eleven years after $200,000 was spent on a consultant who gave the company direction to go forward. Prior to that time the company thrived for over ninety years just by getting ideas from the homegrown officers who had come up through the ranks and served the company well without the outside influence. It was an amazing process to see the consultant devise a whole portfolio of questions for both the salespeople and clients of this company and go around the whole country asking, researching, and recording.

I was one of those interviewed. I had been telling this home office my feelings on these matters for ten years prior to the time the genius came to interview me. My information was free and not in accordance with his ultimate findings. I feel the company could have gotten the same data from its sales force and its customers without paying such an exorbitant stipend. I did complain about the process and said the information was available all the time just for the listening. I was told that I was right but the consultant's report indicated some lateral moves for some top echelon executives and proper decorum would indicate that no jealousy or rivalry dictated these changes. It was all good, clean, objective reasoning that caused the realignment. This was The Consultant Syndrome at its zenith.

The Meeting Syndrome

"Let's have a meeting." It rolls off the tongue like so much poetry that it hardly seems anything at all is happening. There are meetings for every thing one could imagine. Meetings to set agendas, budgets, territories, finances, future meeting dates, and anything that connotes rule by committee instead of commitment. It's easy to call a meeting. I can't think of a bigger time waster.

Also, it's a great way to stay away from work and the telephone calls one doesn't want to take. Just have the secretary say the person is in a meeting or, in the refined terms of the lawyer, "He's in conference." Usually at meetings there is one king chicken and all the rest of the hens. One person is dominant and calling all of the shots but it is reworked so it seems that some sniff of democracy is evident. In other words, most meetings are not necessary; the decision has already been made but the stamp of approval and anonymity is needed. Therefore, the meeting is called.

"The Meeting Syndrome" is a real stamp of approval. "The masses vote for themselves what they cannot earn for themselves." Usually the course of action is firmly implanted in someone's mind before the meeting ever takes place. But in accordance with The Consultant Syndrome if the meeting is successful, the king chicken can take the credit for having called the meeting or having been the chairperson. If the meeting is unsuccessful, it can be blamed on the committee.

I was once in the home office of a major insurance company having lunch with the top brass in the officer's dining room. We had a table for six and one of the diners was a junior vice-president who had just returned from a trip into the field. He told of his bad experience with a large hotel in Chicago where they would not accept his commercial traveler's discount card, saying they did not have the company on record. They did have the mortgage department of this same company on their list but not the head office, per se. He argued but to no avail and ended up paying the tourist rate.

The discussion was meaningless and it seemed to me there were a number of things that could be done now that he was back in his own office. One of the officers said that, perhaps, a letter should go to the hotel letting them know that the mortgage department, which had the same name as the parent company, was identical and a card should be listed in the name of the department as well as the parent. Another suggestion was that a card be applied for in the name of the home office, in addition to the one that already existed. This could be done by letter since no one would be going to Chicago in the next few months. These both seemed like good suggestions to me but the truth of the matter was that it was the most frivolous type of table talk which could be solved either by phone or letter, simply and quickly. None of it made any real difference and it seemed to me that all this high-priced talent should have been discussing matters of more importance to the hundreds of thousands of policyholders.

Here is how it ended. It was a grand-slam as it combined a number of syndromes; The 41 Memo, The Consultant, The Committee (which we haven't come to yet) and The Meeting Syndromes. The top officer at the table listened carefully but did not commit himself while the others romanced the subject. Then he spoke with authority and finality when he said, "Jim, you meet with Phil, then meet with Mark in the mortgage department and see how they got their card. Prepare an agenda, and call a meeting to discuss it fully." End of discussion. End of lunch. Everyone stood up and left the table while I sat there trying to figure out if this was business or welfare.

The Committee Syndrome

Harry Truman one said, "The buck stops here." In most corporate situations it takes a long time for the buck to stop. It keeps going from place to place because no one is willing to take any semblance of responsibility. On the corporate level this is known as The Committee Syndrome. However, it also filters down to the individual level where it is known as, "That's not my department." There must be something good about the large corporate way of doing business because it seems to work. Yet one has to wonder how since it appears there is so much wasted personnel.

When dealing with a large corporation, just like dealing with a small one, somebody sometimes has to make a decision; who or when depends upon what committee the particular issue befalls. Each committee operates like a little company of its own. It has a budget of its own and is required to account for that money and time. The last item mentioned is fuzzy since it takes into consideration all of the previously mentioned syndromes and a few not yet mentioned. It would be sinful for the budget committee to know what the finance committee or the operations committee was doing. Each will know eventually but not until the report comes out properly fattened for good authenticity; the thicker the better.

Most likely in a really large corporation, this is the best and most efficient way to work. However, in a medium size corporation, or even the larger ones, there are too many committees and too much time is wasted while waiting for one committee to speak so that another can act or react. It's frightful to fall through the cracks when requesting information or service from one of these committee orientated companies. One can get lost or disheartened before he or she gets the answer. Then there are those within these companies who delight in saying, "We can't do anything until it's through the whatever committee." Congress is a good example of this. There are more committees than are needed, for sure. All forms of government operate on the basis of committees. There are "Blue Ribbon" committees appointed for the purpose of selecting a blue ribbon committee.

I once had an idea which affected some insurance legislation in the state of Michigan. I wrote to the committee head who was in charge of the action. I received a letter which praised my foresight and energy in taking the time to write and make observations. I was told that my ideas were of value and a committee would be formed to look into them. I responded by saying that if the state of Michigan, in over one hundred years of statehood, did not already have a committee or department to handle the minor suggestions I made regarding the pending action, my idea was a bad one and I requested that it be withdrawn. I went further to say that if committee action was needed, it was OK to form one only if two other already existing ones were disbanded. I never received a further response and I don't know what happened to my idea.

Government is know for forming committees. The responsibility and accountability for an action can then be shared so the job is made to look important. This way a lot of featherbedding and cushy positions can be continued. Getting rid of a government committee is like getting rid of a "temporary" tax. Some of these committee meetings are held in secret and take long intervals to complete. The public can't question what is secret or unintelligible when the meeting is completed. Government is not alone in this syndrome. I often wonder what our profit statements would look like if all of the waste were eliminated. I'm not intimating that all committees are wasteful, but the majority are suspect. Take as an example of overstaffing the astounding runaround of the Chrysler Corporation in the early 1980's. Lee Iacocca was under orders to cut his white collar staff by fifty percent in order to qualify for government backing for the gigantic bailout loans.

Some committees become a job within a job. There are those who have duties other than to be a member of some select committee. Yet for unknown reasons the committee work seems to grow in inverse proportion to the productive output of those committees. A good way to avoid an issue is to blame it on the committee. It is easy to say that an action cannot be done because a certain step is still locked in committee. And like ants at a picnic, committees beget committees. When a decision is near more information is needed and, rather than getting it quickly without reinventing the wheel, a subcommittee is formed.

It's the American way. Unfortunately, it is a very costly American way of goofing off. It costs both time and money and there ain't anything else that we got. I suspect there must be half of our working force that is truly bored with their work and find The Committee Syndrome is just one more way to pass the time.

The Report Syndrome

Another way to keep business in a state of retardation is The Report Syndrome. This one has most of the negative attributes of the others but the object here is time delay and passing the buck. An offshoot of this syndrome is The 41 Memo Syndrome and we'll cover both of these at the same time.

We do too darn many reports. Most of what is said in ten pages can be said in ten words, recorded by a secretary and sent around to those affected in an official memo, or other useful correspondence.

The reason I referred to The 41 Memo Syndrome here is because we covered memos earlier and I only wanted to touch on those as part of the Report philosophy. So many of these business retardation processes are intertwined that they look like they are part of one another, but that is not always the case. However, The Report Syndrome does contain all of the others. Another way of slowing up or disguising work by any of the other methods can be further sullied by putting them in writing. This truly looks more official since the written word means someone actually took some time and did the research and the work. It may have also involved someone else because some typing had to be done.

Most of these procedures are interdependent upon each other once The Report Syndrome is invoked. The veracity looks more complete when it is in writing. Reports are tougher than some of the others because they usually involve deadlines. When I hear some harried executive say he has to work late at night finishing a report, I don't know whether to feel sorry for him or her because of the great deal of overwork, or feel disdain because he or she has let the work slide until the last minute.

For sure, there are mostly legitimate needs for reports in business; after all, there is the need to know what is going on. However, I think all will agree there is too much of the "White Fog" going on in business and it isn't to promote what *is* happening, but is for the purpose of hiding what *hasn't* happened. What person, intent upon doing a proper job, can sincerely read, understand, retain, and make use of all the reports and memos that transverse his or her desk? I have seen instances of department heads giving verbal results of ongoing projects and heard their superiors quickly spit out, "Send me a report." In most of those situations, the project had not been completed or was not important enough to take the time to write lengthy tomes about the goings-on.

I have no way of verifying this and I don't know if it was said in jest but I heard a radio commentator say that the Big Three auto makers process more paper than they do steel. I wouldn't doubt it.

Many of these reports are only an extension of the person's English classes. Remember the days when you had to make up a short story for class? That was one of the greatest preparations for real life business for, in reality, that's what most of the reports are; made up short stories. The greatest example of this is the script writing that goes into the most important of financial reports—the expense account. This is when all the corners of one's imagination come into play. I have said to friends of mine who are in businesses where they have an expense account, "Take me to lunch only once out of five times when you turn in my name on your voucher." I say it as a job but I usually get a surprised, incredulous look.

To illustrate the uselessness of some of these reports, I refer to the sales reports that are required of young salespeople. I, for one, think they are absolutely vital and should be done exactly, accurately, and timely. So many of the novices in selling, though, don't agree with that philosophy and think completing the reports is a complete waste of time. On occasion, they are right if the supervisors do not study them, interpret them and put them to practical use. Too many salespeople absolutely fake their reports. It works for a while and for some it may work forever. In this instance, the salesperson is only hurting him/herself. Those reports are the lifeline of their success if they would only use them properly. I read a *Parade* magazine article which listed the top ten reasons for business failures. Before reading the article, I would have guessed undercapitalization would have been the chief culprit. The article, using official census statistics, cited inadequate records as the primary reason for business failure. The message is "If you don't know where you are going, how do you know when you get there?"

That's Not My Department Syndrome

We now come to one of the most important of business functions: the department. This is the only real way to make any profit; specialize and get the economy of scale. To that end, we departmentalize. Along with the formation of departments comes the excuse, "That's not my department." The quickest example of this, that I can think of, is the telephone call to city hall when you need something done. You may just as well start the conversation off with the words, "I know this isn't your department, but . . ."As soon as one makes a request from a unit of government the knee jerk reaction is, "That's not my department."

Along with the department dodge come the telephone switch. It is then possible to spend a whole day being switched from unit to unit, staying on hold for interminable periods, and repeating the problem or request to everyone who gets on the phone. They all listen to everything before they say it, "That's not my department; I'll switch you." I once called my local government to inform them of a cavernous pothole in the road near my home. I was switched about three times until I found an attentive ear who then said to me, "Is that hot patch or cold patch?"

The reason a lot of this stalling goes on over the phone is because it is hard to identify a voice without a name. I always try to get a name even though the parties are sometimes reluctant. I have even had people tell me that is information they don't have to give out. For those who are of that ilk, the departmentalization is a great way to goof-off.

On occasion, it is legitimate that the workers don't know the function of their departments. It is easy to move work along by using the "flow through" method. One can look awfully busy by just shuffling things and phone calls while at the same time be doing nothing except looking active. Some projects actually fall into more than one department, in which case there should be more than one interested party. But if the wrong ones are involved the work load becomes doubled instead of halved. Murphey's Law say, "What can go wrong, will." To some strict loafers, Murphey was an optimist.

This syndrome is also typified by the phrase "killing time." It sure is the opposite of, "To kill time, try working it to death."

The Supervisor Syndrome

Bosses and supervisors are important; someone has to take the responsibility for the big picture. In all of life there is good and there is bad. This section is a sardonic look at our little foibles in what we sometimes mistakenly call "work."

There are good supervisors and there are bad supervisors. Some work and some don't. I'm fascinated when I sometimes see persons in positions of responsibility who are the chief liabilities of an efficient organization. I wonder what they do and how they got into a position of high compensation and authority. I make no fun of the good supervisors, but the ones who are in positions of authority and merely clog up the lanes are a pitiful lot.

For the bad ones the main job seems to be to get the credit for all the good things that happen and to keep a low profile, or no profile at all, when the going gets rough. Upper management is not faultless in the selection of unworthy supervisors. The purpose of business is sales. Every business in the world is a sales venture, including those who are in the service aspect of business. Every worker in the world is a salesperson, selling either goods or services. Those who have products to peddle are easily recognized. Those who indicate they are not "sales" people are one hundred percent wrong. I offer the example of a dentist. Even though there is no tangible product for the dentist to sell, he or she is selling the ability to pull a tooth at so much per extraction, or fill a tooth at so much per cavity. Service is what is being sold in this instance. The same reasoning holds true for lawyers, judges, paper shufflers, and all the other jobs and professions.

Using this reasoning about everyone being a salesperson, those who get really good at it should be left in their jobs to further themselves and become even more productive and proficient. That's not the feeling of many companies. Some use the philosophy of taking the good salespeople and "promoting" them into supervisory work. The feeling is they can spread themselves wider by teaching and overseeing the dissemination of the good traits. In most cases this does not work well. A really good teacher should remain a teacher; a really good salesperson should remain so. There is no sound evidence that says because someone can handle a job well they can also teach and manage that job well for other people.

Therefore, we often have situations of supervisors being in the way of efficient workers. Good employees are 98% perspiration and 2% inspiration. It has always worked that way so it is not nice to fool with Mother Nature and try to change everybody. It would be a far smarter move to find the skills of the employee and nurture them along the same road on which they are already travelling and cater to what is already in place. The problems come when The Supervisor Syndrome is combined with some of the others and good, productive people get turned off by having to conform to ironcast rules which stifles freethinking. Thomas Jefferson said, "That government governs best which governs least." The same is true in business. So many supervisors get in the way just to try to justify their positions. The best way to answer the question, "Who's in charge here?" is to say, "Everyone." If all do their job with any modicum of dedication, everyone will get the credit and there will be a need for more employees on every level because the business will prosper.

The Fifteen Percent Syndrome

There is an unwritten law of business growth. If some executives of large, multibranched companies were to be transferred from city to city, they could function without missing a stroke. All one has to say at the first executive meeting is, "What we need this year is a fifteen percent increase." It bodes well because it is double figures, it is not as low as ten percent (which seems small) and not as large as twenty percent (which may seem grabby) and may, in fact, be a hard job to do.

There are also sales vice-presidents or large corporations who do not know or care what the product of the company is. They are adept at looking at the lists of cities where the company operates and seeing the production. To these types of people who care nothing about anything except climbing the corporate ladder, nothing else makes any difference. The customers or employees or products or services don't matter. The number one job is to look good in the charts and darts. For some, this is tougher to do these days with the all-exposing computer. It's tougher to fudge the records when the computer spills all in a tick.

These types of people don't know if the product is steel or insurance. They could be blindfolded on Friday and taken to a new location in a new industry on Monday morning. The first request would be to see a list of the production of the various locations. Without asking or caring about why the numbers are as they are, they could easily say, "What we need is a fifteen percent increase." No one can argue with the new guru and he or she has a full year of grace to make the figures. The fact that the current list will be a pretty true indicator of consistent performance, with the usual variants because of circumstances in different parts of the country, makes no difference.

So when I run across one of these individuals who has no soul other than the graphs, I handle myself with a cold "numbers only" attitude. In response to their questions about how business is, and knowing they love the percentage game, I respond with the non-sensical, "I'm tripling my decreases."

The Now Changing Syndrome

Every so often the individual customer, or anyone else dealing with a large corporation, will come up with a complaint or idea that is absolutely correct and defies opposition. If it doesn't fit into one of the syndromes I have already mentioned there is a catchall category that blocks the customer's further complaint. This one is a masterstroke. It is known as The Now Changing Syndrome. When the moment of truth arrives and the winner is the customer, he or she very often hears the good news-bad news response, "You are right and we're now changing it."

That is almost irrefutable. The company is saying you are correct and they are on your side but there is nothing to be done right now. The period of time until the desired action is instituted is unknown and depends on all the other syndromes. It is hard to be angry with someone who is on your side. It is a great way to get rid of something that irritates the supplier right now. The questioner could go further by asking when it will be changed and the answer would make absolutely no difference because that is later and the issue does not have to be faced right now. The responder could say, "I don't know," and the conversation would end. The answer could be, "Within a few months." The seeker has no choice but to back off. The answer could have been any other indefinite time and he or she would have had to retreat. The point was won; now it is strictly a matter of timing.

The timing could be like operating with the government and having a cost overrun. All that is needed is an update. Any further inquiries could be answered just the same, "You're right and we're now changing it."

This ploy is another way to get out of current work or responsibility. How to change it? I don't know but I'm working on it right now.

The Spend The Money Syndrome

This is a good one and defies all economic logic. Have you ever heard the plaint, "The money is there and if we don't spend it, it will have to go back." This is a common government or zero based budget phenomenon. I read about this a lot in the paper. Here's how it works: a department has a budget with a certain amount of money. To some minds this means that it must be spent. If there were more funds left, on paper, when the time frame was nearing a close, there would be a panic to spend the money or it would "have to go back." This is the tough part to understand but the obvious questions are the ones that any freshman journalism student would ask: who, what, when, where, why.

In life, or in one's personal finances, if money isn't spent, it is saved. But when it comes to the company checkbook or a government program of transfer payments, too many people are the quickest draws in the West. There is an overriding fear that the money will disappear into space if every cent, tentatively allocated, is not used. This syndrome is enhanced when there is a cost overrun because, to the lame thinker, nothing went back. To the same gouger's logic, all is right with the world because matter can neither be created nor destroyed. There was no expense in blowing the money just to waste it. It would have been sinful to allow it to be available at some other time when it was more direfully needed. There has to be a warped sense of values to spend money just because it appeared as a paper projection. The thinking has to be that it was not the property of the spender and, therefore, had no personal effect. Some people think it is impossible for the government or a corporation to have an effect on them in the final accounting. It is almost the same reasoning used by the person who commits insurance fraud. He or she sets out to swindle the rest of the insureds with the weak thinking that the insurance companies have so much money this pittance will have no effect. This person further leans to the conclusion that the company's money is not the policyholder's money. It baffles me to see this kind of thinking without the realization that, ultimately, it will show up in everyone's premium.

The person who uses the idea of spending the money for the same reason that adventurers climb Mt. Everest—because it is there—is as much of a cheat as the one who deliberately sets out to steal from the company. Money wasted now isn't available when it may be more sorely needed. However, don't try to discuss this with the culprits. They will never comprehend the logic and will only further frustrate you with the response, "Everybody does it."

The Do It Yourself Syndrome

There was a time, not too many years ago, when you would go to the gasoline station and get all kinds of service and other goodies to take with you. You would get your gas (for 20 cents a gallon, but that's another story and another syndrome) a glass with a picture of your home National Football League team, some trading stamps, a chance in a contest to win a trip to some exotic spot, and $1,000,000 in cash. The attendant would wipe your windshield, fill the tank, check under the hood, and say, "Thank you."

Most important to all of this was the fact you never stepped out of your car and you were served by a station attendant. If the station were busy and you even made an attempt to pump your own gas, you had better watch yourself because someone might have come after you with a monkey wrench. There was a certain mystique about those pumps and it required someone with a mechanical knowledge to use them, or such was the attitude conveyed by the providers. If you did touch the pump, someone would appear quickly and ask snidely, "In a hurry?"

Times have changed. Now, the gas jockeys are a dying breed since most stations do not have any. If you do come across a station with full service, it is easy to see the worth of the helper. The difference per gallon between doing it yourself and having it done to you is about 30 cents. Fairly substantial, I would say. The gas is the same and your car may not require anything under the hood except the look into it, but the price tag for the pampering is easily determined by looking at the difference between the price on the left pump and the price on the right pump.

Times do change. I remember the days before we had super-markets. I know for some people it will be an impossibility to even imagine there was a place where someone else did the picking off the shelves and completed the order of one person before waiting on another. Now, the hypermarkets sell not only food but auto parts, banking services, lottery tickets, photo developing, shoe repairs and, soon to come, insurance and financial services. The thing which makes it possible is doing it all yourself, from making the selection and carrying the goods to the checkpoint so a clerk can run the items over a scanner which will automatically list the purchases and total the bill. If the counter person talks or says, "Thank you" you can consider yourself as having had a good day.

The telephone used to be the most stable of utilities. It seemed like it worked faultlessly forever. If service was required, one phone call brought a repair person to the house almost instantaneously. The individual usually fixed the instrument quickly or left you a loaner phone while your own was out of the home or business. There was no extra charge and all the phone user had to do was make a call to report the problem. These days, when one reports trouble, one is told the repair person will be out within the next two days and only between the hours of nine and five. The service charge will be very high per hour after a minimum base.

Or, if the troubled party desired, the phone could be brought to a convenient phone center and left for repair or replaced for a fee.

Another product of the changing times is the personal ownership of phones on a very reasonable basis. There is even the choice that can be made to dump the errant instrument and replace it with a new "communication center." These are more examples of "do it yourself."

Who would have ever dreamed of the days when you could get money out of the bank at an hour when it was closed. Only John Dillinger and Jesse James were able to do that. Now, if you choose, you can conduct a very active banking practice without ever being in the place or ever seeing a teller or manager. Times change and most of these are for the better, but there are other areas where the lack of service or the supposed economy of scale has drastic results.

The combination of any of the other syndromes which I have named or all of them taken together are included in The Do It Yourself Syndrome. One way or another, when service people do not do their jobs or are not accountable for their actions, the task is kicked back to the consumer or another worker for them to do. It has happened to all financial industries and ours is no exception. For instance, in the stock market, it is possible to install a computer terminal in your home and conduct active trading just by going from the bedroom to the computer room. This is a voluntary action and does not fall precisely into the area which I am addressing. Yet, the point is we are able to or are forced to take on more and more of our own required needs, sometimes even if we are paying someone else to do the service.

The large home offices of all corporations, including the insurance companies, have placed all their sales forces on a "do it yourself" basis without even announcing it to the field. Please don't take the last statement to mean there is any less paper going to the sales force. The field information bulletins keep coming in tidal wave fashion. They keep promising newer and improved services and systems but, unfortunately, all of them are not true. Some turn out to be wishful thinking of what would like to be done and what could be done by the use of modern systems. But the gorge between the real and the promised is deep and wide.

The computer explosion and the mystery that goes with it has allowed for real and imagined excuses for not doing work to proliferate and become impossible to challenge or disprove. The saying, "It's in the computer and there is nothing that can be done until it comes out," has become the watchword of the lazy employee. I am amazed when I get a note or a phone call telling me something will take an indefinite period longer because it has to be done "by hand." This implies that doing something by hand should take longer than doing it by machine. I grant you that is correct when the process has actually started, but if the machine is not working or is emboweled with something else, doing the task by hand wins easily.

Some employees have never done certain functions by hand and would have to be reprogrammed to do a little thinking on their own. They lose sight of the fact there is a client or customer waiting for a service and that should be their main thrust, not getting the right paper in the right slot with the right color on the right pile. By the way, I would be happy with some of the delays if it resulted in getting things in the right pile or the right place.

Another astounding feature of the computer explosion is the excuse which says the file is lost. This is announced with a haughty air and it is expected that the excuse will be accepted and the one who requested the service will go away and not be a bother anymore.

Big business and big diversions into other ventures have caused companies to confuse employees. They don't know if they work for the parent company or the offspring division. This also has led to the hindering of services and undue delays in getting previously efficient procedures into the arguable zone. Getting policies issued can sometimes take half a year. The files get lost and the attending physician's statements get lost more frequently than in the not too distant past. Employees are quick to use the excuse of any of the earlier syndromes. The result is the agent becomes a detective trying to reconstruct what happened to the application or the beneficiary change form once it left his or her office. This, too, adds to the unannounced policy of do it yourself.

It seems like the accountability level is on empty. Few people are willing to get involved beyond the boundaries of their own desk which is in line with The Animal Kingdom Syndrome. There has been a noticeable drop in the credibility level of the insurance agent in recent times. He or she may fight all day long with the home office to get something straightened out then have to gloss over the problem with the client while reporting why there are unacceptable delays taking place. The agent must do this without besmirching the name of the company which, in turn, will besmirch the attitude about the agent at the same time.

It also seems like certain requested services are completely forgotten unless there is a constant follow-up on the part of the agent. Things are always getting shoved aside and they would remain there if not for a constant jarring monitoring. There is no question we have lost the sharp cutting edge off the main concern at which we were good in the past—service.

We are in both a product and service industry. The products are multiplying like coat hangers but the service is taking a corresponding dip. What is holding it together is the sales force which still works on a commission basis. The proliferation of products in the last five years has taken some of the credibility away from us as agents. Many are feeding off themselves and their competition. This does not leave a favorable impression in the minds of the clientele even though they are eager to take advantage of a replacement situation which looks like a good deal for them. However, when we add to this the problems which are currently permeating the entire service side of our industry, we are losing ground. Many of us have to spend a great portion of our time covering up for service mistakes and omissions which should not be occurring. We are doing it ourselves; that is, things which are not normally our function and things about which we were not concerned just a few years ago.

There is the old adage which says if you want a job done well, do it yourself. Nevertheless, because of the omission of service or delays in service "do it yourself" has, unwittingly, become the norm. This is not an efficient way to run a business. We are taught to delegate but it is not practical in some cases where the service is not being done. Delegation would be the road to termination if the agent did not get involved himself or herself.

We live in an era of cost-cutting consciousness and economy of scale. The way to profit is more production for less overhead. This is why businesses hire time control experts and efficiency specialists. Some of the kickback of services to the field representatives is purposely and some is unwittingly. Some businesses do it silently without telling the sales force there will be reductions in services. It just happens that departments are merged and previous services are cut short. Then, silently in this fashion, tasks which were handled by the main offices are strung out in time or delayed to the point where anxious, needy salespeople do it themselves.

This may be the trend of the times. Business always changes as I mentioned in a previous syndrome. Perhaps we are coming to the era of the field force pumping the gas themselves. If it were announced and if the method of payment were forthcoming, there would be less howling from the men and women on the front line and the customers they serve. But, in too many instances, it is a silent movement only understood when the deadlines are immediate. It is like the crime problem in most of our major cities. We are tolerating more crime now than we did ten years ago or even five years ago. We hear so much about stealing, plundering, and other sordid misdeeds that we take a certain amount of it for granted. We know it is going to happen. We just hope it stays away from us and, when the scoring statistics are written, our names are not on the police victim's blotter. To this end, there is a lot more self-policing and self-protection going on today than there was in the past. Gun sales and alarm sales are escalating.

The same analogy may be true for salespeople. We have to protect ourselves and our clients from the loss of services, so The Do It Yourself Syndrome becomes an involuntary part of everyday business.

There are many more syndromes. Business is funny and, at the same time, serious. It balances itself in relation to the input and output levels. The syndromes and patterns will go on and so will successful salespeople who continue to do the basics. Maybe it will go a little smoother because of an understanding of the syndromes presented in this chapter.

4

What's in a Name

A Different Standard

We have all heard the old maxim, "Price is no object." I had a case where this was exactly the situation. The price of the insurance made absolutely no difference; as the case turned out, the label on the policy was the only criterion. I sold a policy in June, 1981, on the life of Harry. He was in his early fifties and the premium for the $200,000 of graded premium life should have been $4,700 on a standard basis, for the first year. Due to health reasons, the policy was issued with an elevated premium of $5,300, for the first year. It was not an easy case to deliver but, after much of the negotiations which occur on these situations had been resolved, he accepted the policy and wrote a check for the annual premium.

In January, 1982, I received a notice from the carrier that a replacement form had been completed for this policy, by another agent representing another company. The reason listed for considering the replacement was the attempt to receive a "standard" issue. I called the policyholder to discuss the proceedings and he once again relayed to me his feelings about having to pay a health extra. I told him that, in time, the present carrier would consider dropping the extra charge. I also pointed out that the projected standard premium as listed on the replacement form was larger than the total premium he was now paying by about $1,000. He indicated to me he knew that but wanted a standard policy. He also told me the other agent had called and said he already had approval for the policy, although it was not yet in his agency. As usual, for whatever reasons imaginable, the replacement forms were delayed in getting to me and the exam and other requirements were so far along that the policy was near issue.

I told him that I would go back to the original carrier and ask them to consider any updated facts but the policyholder said he wanted to do business with the person who got him the standard contract. I suggested we would have time to meet since the premium renewal date was not until June and it was now only January. He responded by saying he had already given the entire annual amount to the other company. I reminded him that this would give him $400,000 of newly issued insurance and the estate planning interviews only indicated a need for $200,000. I also pointed out that he was now paying an extra half-year's premium to get the tag "standard" next to his name. In addition, the standard premium of the second company was $1,000 more than the special premium of the first company. I might also add that the sale was not an easy one and I thought I had done a pretty good job of doing the analysis and getting a check for what was the proper solution.

All of this made no difference to him. He told me he had already paid for the insurance and was going to accept the policy as soon as it was delivered. I tried further to show the waste of premium dollars since the extra premium policy, even though lower on a straight-up basis, had more cash values all the way down the schedule, even though he was also losing a year in age.

Needless to say, I lost the case. What made it even stranger was the fact that I had also sold a policy on his wife during the estate planning sessions. That one is still in force and he admits it is a better contract than the one he purchased from the second company. He also admits the rated policy is a better one than the standard one, even after a year and with a different company. The only thing that made any difference to him was not to be called anything but "standard."

For a TV script, one could not think of anything stranger than this case but I suppose it proves that truth is stranger than fiction. At the same time, it shows if you stick in this business long enough, anything can happen. The good part of that moral is the consideration of having a large enough book of business so there is sufficient exposure to have some strange things happen to you. None of us are immune to any weird circumstance. Selling brings them all out; volume smooths them out.

The last little story on labels shows what a title denotes to some people. This man was concerned with having a standard issue policy, not the cost of the coverage. Too often, we are the ones who lead to the confusion. When I refer to "we" I include all segments of the life insurance marketing system. First and foremost, the culprits are marketing department people who give names to policies. We live in an era of "new and improved." The deodorants and soaps on TV are constantly bellowing at the audience that they have forty percent more of some new "DpLm3" or sixty percent less of "harmful Thridens." They may also tell us they have no caffeine in their latest deodorant and they give us twenty percent less wrapping paper. You can buy laundry soap that makes green bubbles but won't hurt the atmosphere. The deodorants, as well as the soap, rarely change; the advertisements provide all of the hogwash. The Borax commercials, however, do their job; they sell. People like change even if it is only touted but not factual.

The advertising agencies or departments of the insurance companies have not missed this reaction. With the proliferation of products and services of the 1980's, there also came the onslaught of advertising peddling policies by name alone. The names ring with energy and challenge. We now have titles such as "Challenger," "Incredible Life," "Inedible Life," "Ultrasonic Life," "Magic Life," "Challenger 2," "Incredible 2," "Current Assumption Life," "Current Consumption Life," "Son of Current Consumption Life," and so forth. The next generation of policies will probably follow the trend of car advertising and be named after animals. How about a "Python CSO 80," or a "Sabre Tiger Modified Twelve"?

That's all poking a bit of fun at where we are today but there is truth in the premise that we have confused the public. Now when I say "we" I speak of the agent, too. We go out and stick to the fancy acronym which comes with the computer disc (formerly rate book) and we really expect our clientele to understand the difference between any of those two monstrosities I just named above. We are just as much to blame as anyone else in the marketing chain if we do not make our propositions crystal clear to our prospects. When we go in with names which are "Madison Avenue slick," maybe the customer should think it over longer or get two estimates. Maybe there is two much sizzle and not enough steak. Or, possibly, with all that sizzle, the buyer doesn't even know there is a steak involved.

Illustration 4-1 which follows is a classic and serves as the basis for a style which I have developed. The premise is to use words which attract the client and make him or her want to see the whole illustration. They must not give in to preconceived notions regarding insurance plans before even seeing the whole presentation. I am speaking of the propensity to assume term is better than whole life and to close one's mind to seeing the attributes of both philosophies.

About ten years ago, I gave up the use of the words "term" and "permanent" when illustrating insurance policies. I realized there were too many preconceptions that went with the words. On some occasions, if I only showed a permanent policy, questions concerning term insurance would be asked. Then, no matter how erudite my language might be, I found the client had to defend his ideas against mine. No matter what I said, I was backtracking. If the client started to agree with me, it was easy and even reasonable for him or her to say, "Let's start with the term, and I'll change later." Now, where this is the right solution, I have no quarrel with the idea and probably will be the one to suggest it.

I reasoned, was it really the name of the policy we were selling, or was it what the policy would do? The vital statistics were face amount, premium, and cash value. If we never tell the prospect the name of the plan, how can he or she object to the idea that does him the most good, no matter what it is called? Our actuaries and marketing committees are great. I've made my share of actuary jokes, but I legitimately admire and respect our "numbers" men and women. I trust them when I quote a rate. I have no way of making the calculations, and I find it very convenient to go to a rate book or to a machine and get a quote.

I know every insurance plan must have a name—the state insurance department require it—but if we looked in any book and started a list of 100 names, we'd be astounded by the poetry that goes into a financial package called a policy. When we give it serious thought we, as agents, truly are to be complimented for explaining the attributes of some of the fancy acronyms we use for policies. As I mentioned previously, sometimes it's no wonder the prospect says he or she wants to think it over. He isn't dumb, but he might appear so if he accepted all the fancy prose we use without even questioning it.

In Illustration 4-1, the need was $150,000 of key person insurance on the son of a longtime client. The boy had just graduated from college and was entering his dad's business. The $150,000 amount was arrived at to coincide with the intended value of the stock Bob would receive as a gift from his father in the next few years. The insurance was to be a key man asset now, then switched to a stock redemption format when necessary. In effect, if was a future option sale.

Frank, the father, was one of the policyowners with whom I had grown. His first policy, in 1957, had a $7,000 face amount; now the premiums are triple that. The need was firmly fixed, so the purpose now was to place the best-suited policy. I felt that stringing the whole 44 years to age 65 would be very effective in showing the progression, or regression, of premiums. The first two columns are self-explanatory. The third column shows premiums for five-year renewable term. That's what we were showing a few years ago; on average, the premiums beat yearly renewable term, at that time. Presently, we know it is a whole new ball game in the term field. The fourth column illustrates a policy that consists of nearly seventy percent permanent as basic insurance, and about thirty percent term, which automatically converts itself within the policy by use of dividends. In this way it always remains at the full face amount. Some companies call these contracts "Extraordinary Life" or "Enhancement." The fourth column could also be used to show nonparticipating insurance. The fifth column shows participating permanent insurance with dividends used to reduce premiums.

When we finished establishing the problem and the solution, I showed this illustration. I explained to the father and son there were three kinds of policies to solve the needs: Increasing Premium; Level Premium or; Decreasing Premium. The Increasing Premium started at a low of $499.50 at age 21 and reached a high of $4,182.00 at age 65. The total premiums to age 65 would be $59,605.50, and the cash value would be zero. The Level Premium started at $1,152.00 and remained constant. By age 65, the total premium would be $50,688.00, and the cash value would be $89,095.00. The Decreasing Premium plan began at a high of $1,902.00 and decreased to a point at age 65, whereby the insurance company would be paying Bob $18 to keep the policy. The total premium would be $34,324.50 and holding, and the cash value would be $85,800.00. Using this kind of display makes it tough to get out the words, "We'll take the Increasing Premium."

The father did have a few questions and they were leading toward the Increasing Premium. I was about to start answering when the son said, "Dad, I can picture myself being your age of 47. Look at the sheet. By 47, we would be paying $1,179 under the Increasing and only $562.50 under the Decreasing." Notice, he skipped the Level Premium in the center column. Apparently, the illustration had made its point, since the discussion was steering toward what I felt was the best policy, Decreasing Premium, Permanent. Also, at this point, I was not doing any selling; young Bob was telling his father all the obvious pluses.

Illustration 4-1

Age 21 **Bob______________** **Face Amount $150,000**

Year	Age	Increasing Premium	Level Premium	Decreasing Premium
1	21	$ 499.50	$ 1,152.00	$ 1,902.00
2	22	499.50	1,152.00	1,902.00
3	23	499.50	1,152.00	1,777.50
4	24	499.50	1,152.00	1,677.00
5	25	499.50	1,152.00	1,587.00
6	26	504.00	1,152.00	1,501.50
7	27	504.00	1,152.00	1,423.50
8	28	504.00	1,152.00	1,354.50
9	29	504.00	1,152.00	1,293.00
10	30	504.00	1,152.00	1,242.00
11	31	531.00	1,152.00	1,188.00
12	32	531.00	1,152.00	1,134.00
13	33	531.00	1,152.00	1,078.50
14	34	531.00	1,152.00	1,029.00
15	35	531.00	1,152.00	1,011.00
16	36	628.50	1,152.00	940.50
17	37	628.50	1,152.00	894.00
18	38	628.50	1,152.00	847.50
19	39	628.50	1,152.00	814.50
20	40	628.50	1,152.00	778.50

21	41	828.00	1,152.00	742.50
22	42	828.00	1,152.00	714.00
23	43	828.00	1,152.00	684.00
24	44	828.00	1,152.00	655.50
25	45	828.00	1,152.00	625.50
26	46	1,179.00	1,152.00	592.50
27	47	1,179.00	1,152.00	562.50
28	48	1,179.00	1,152.00	529.50
29	49	1,179.00	1,152.00	496.50
30	50	1,179.00	1,152.00	463.50
31	51	1,752.00	1,152.00	432.00
32	52	1,752.00	1,152.00	396.00
33	53	1,752.00	1,152.00	364.50
34	54	1,752.00	1,152.00	330.00
35	55	1,752.00	1,152.00	297.00
36	56	2,572.50	1,152.00	262.50
37	57	2,572.50	1,152.00	226.50
38	58	2,572.50	1,152.00	190.50
39	59	2,572.50	1,152.00	156.00
40	60	2,572.50	1,152.00	120.00
41	61	4,182.00	1,152.00	85.50
42	62	4,182.00	1,152.00	51.00
43	63	4,182.00	1,152.00	16.50
44	64	4,182.00	1,152.00	18.00(CR)
TOTALS@65		$59,605.50	$50,688.00	34,324.50
CASH VALUES@65		—0—	89,095.00	85,800.00

As an aside, I should point out that this was rather unique and, since that time, I have learned to place the plan I want to sell in the center column, if I'm showing three choices. With two choices, I have found that placing the desired policy second works best. I don't know the psychology behind all of this. People generally feel better in the middle; they don't like their flanks exposed. In the two choice illustration, just like the department store, people don't like to buy the first thing they are shown.

Getting back to the interview, the father said, "The Decreasing costs four times as much to start."

Bob replied, "But, Dad, you told me this corporation never rents anything, we only buy our machinery. We won't get anything back with the Increasing and we make a $51,000 gain with the Decreasing. It seems like we're only leasing the insurance and paying too much."

I was thinking to myself that I could not have said it any better, so I didn't. I kept silent. Dad said, "You're right, Bob. Burt, we'll take the Decreasing."

This has been the predominant reasoning since I started using this kind of proposal. The logic of the presentation was summed up beautifully by a 21-year-old budding executive. Since that time I have very rarely used the word "term" or "permanent" or any of their pseudonyms. I have developed many variations of this main theme and I will share some of these in the following chapters.

5

As the Price of Gold Falls, The Price of Term Rises

The late 1970's and the early 1980's were truly the age of deregulation. I don't know the exact economical or legal meaning of the word "deregulation" but the only thing I can think of is changing things from the way they were. I also don't know how everything became regulated to the point where it now has to be deregulated, but I guess that is the function of big government. We might refer back to Chapter Three on syndromes. It is one of the functions of big business to become goofy with their size and it is the function of government to be the same. Thomas Jefferson said, "That government governs best which governs least." He was right and the move toward untangling everything proves it. I don't know what he would say if he were around today or even if he would understand what was going on.

The modern day government operates on the theory of waves; that is, a wave to raise taxes then a wave to lower taxes, a wave to inundate us with forms then a wave to "simplify" the reporting. The true thrust of a politician is to change things. It is absolutely astounding to watch two politicos having a debate either on television or in person. I can tell you honestly I could agree with either one. They seem so sincere and so truthful as they recite figures and facts verifying their position. It would be hard to accuse either one of trying to deceive a large audience publicly, especially with the press waiting to print every word. Yet somehow they do disagree with each other although they rarely say it. They don't address the same point in the same conversation even though they are asked the same questions. My impression of a debate is two liars with good vocabularies.

So, with this tug-of-war between the in's and the out's, the only to get the power back is to change something. Unfortunately, this is exactly what takes place in business when the competition of a little darker shade comes into being; change is the catalyst to profit. We have always had competition in our business and it has been good. It has made us sharper and stronger always for the benefit of the policyholders. Our major forms of rate competition were the high side and the low side. On the high side, it was simple. The various companies watched each other carefully so that one who would like to make a massive profit by charging a higher premium was restrained by the thought of losing out to the competitors. On the low side, we had the various state insurance commissions requiring minimum rates which were sufficient to pay claims.

Enter a number of things of the modern era. First, going back a few years, television. This medium can be described as a series of commercials wrapped around a main theme, be it a sporting event, soap opera, game show, or movie. Looking at it from the viewpoint of the advertisers, it really makes no difference what the show is. The only concern is will the audience be large enough to give a good return on the investment. Therefore, television from some quarters is only a forum for sales. The salespeople grab a little corner of our minds by separating the interesting parts of our shows with commercials. Here is where the competition gets rough. There is only a very expensive minute available to make the impression. Notice I did not say make the point, only make an impression. The sponsor does not always tell the truth as evidenced by the frequent incursions of the various government regulators such as the FCC, (Federal Communications Commission) the FTC (Federal Trade Commission) and a few others.

We get romanced with good looking actors and alluring places or scenes. Sometimes it isn't even the product which is sold; it is everything else with only a slight emphasis on the product. For example, think of all the cars which are sold on TV, not because of the car but, because of the pretty girls that are in the car or are attracted by the car. This is known as selling the sizzle and not the steak. Recall that Professor Harold Hill in *The Music Man* was not selling music, he was selling uniforms. He impressed upon the people of River City that they needed a band. Also, a whole laundry tub of underwear gets sold, not because of the quality of the garment but, because of the looks of the ballplayer who models it or the beauty queen who poses seminude. Add to all of this the designer labels and "new and improved" and you have the beginnings of selling in the big leagues.

Going back to our term discussion, other factors started to jump into the equation. One was the high interest earnings of the late 1970's and the early 1980's. For some, this gave further attraction to the adage of "buy term and invest the difference." For certain insurance companies this presented problems for fixed rate policies which could not be adjusted by the use of dividends or excess earnings. Looming big in the term warfare were laws and taxation. The deduction of costs for acquiring term insurance was greater than the deduction for whole life policies. Or was it the other way? It makes no difference because the money manipulators found a way to make one look like the other through the use of Madison Avenue tactics. They changed the names of the products by use of "new and improved." Names such as "Increasing Premium Whole Life" and others started to resemble the new line of autos and not life insurance at all.

So the government jumped back in and took over the regulation once again with MODCO, TEFRA (Tax Equity and Fiscal Responsibility Act) and other legislations. The more they regulate, the more there is to deregulate later. This perpetuates a cycle for the politically ambitious and keeps a good thing going.

The rates went down substantially during this period of high interest earning and the public thought they were getting a bargain. Term sales soared as the rest of the product line plunged, all the while the price of gold went up. When the interest rates started to decline and the price of gold started to drop, the risk taking rate makers discovered short-term gains had no place in long-term investments. Reinsurers pulled in their horns and products which had safety values, such as "guaranteed" or "current" rates, and started to become less venturesome. Certain companies with difficulties merged with other stronger sisters and a saner sense of direction settled in. Incidentally, at the same time a couple of annuity companies owned by conglomerates had serious difficulties and rocked the solid, stoic insurance reputation.

The result of it all is that the federal government is looking at our industry with a scrutinizing eye that was previously cast in other areas. We will all pay for the money-grabbing attitudes of some of the gambling entrepreneurs of our business. I remember from my high school studies a law called the Sherman Anti-Trust Act of the 1860's, among others which had to do with forestalling monopolies and price fixing. Just reread the financial pages from any day in the 1970's and the 1980's and try to equate that with the mergers, consolidations, and takeovers which occur every day between some of the largest companies on earth. So many of them are playing Monopoly for whole industries that I wonder if the old laws have been repealed. This is opposite to what appears to be happening with the banks, airlines and telephone companies due to deregulation. We're in line for deregulation and where we will fall ten or twenty years, or even one year, from now is impossible to say.

One thing that has not been repealed or deregulated is that of salesmen and saleswomen selling life insurance in a one-on-one, face-to-face basis. No matter what goes on in the big picture, for the majority of us, the action goes on each day with us sitting on one side of the desk or table and the prospect on the other. Therefore, the ones who care about the clients will find the clients care about them and they will listen to the story of insurance as it fits the individual's needs. Although I do not have any economic theorem to prove the price of gold and term insurance are related, I think they are and I present the rule we all know: "In the long run, if there ain't no insurance, there ain't no gold or nothing else."

For the remainder of this chapter I will share with you some illustrations which have developed as a result of the original "Increasing-Level-Decreasing Premium" proposal you saw in Chapter Four. Most of them will be a comparison of term and permanent plans, although there will be a host of variations. My object with these slimmed down illustrations is to get the prospect to pay attention and hear the whole story before jumping to the conclusion that the lowest price today is the best forever. There is only so much juice in the orange. If something looks too good to be true, it probably isn't. There is no such thing as a free lunch and the tab will be presented someday.

There is also no such thing as a rate book anymore. I know they are still printed but they are obsolete even before they are delivered into the salesperson's hands and they are inflexible after that. The modern way is by computer disc and you can run your own proposal or have it done at the agency. This gives you at least four sheets of paper for every policy you wish to show and gives the client more to "want to think over." I don't have the ledger sheets run since it is the only way to get all the numbers which I need to figure what I want to show. My philosophy is to demonstrate that which is important in a fashion which the viewer can fully understand.

I have the full displays with me during the interviews and I ask the prospect if he or she would prefer the full four pounds of confetti, or the summary sheet of the plans. We still have laws and other regulations to observe so I am always certain to eventually give the full proposal to the client or his or her professional advisor. I also make sure I have the plan which was selected in my file.

Illustration 5-1 is a comparison between Yearly Renewable Term and 15-Year Graded Premium Life. I know what the plans are from the code I put at the bottom of the two columns. This is necessary because in future year's reference to this proposal I want to be able to precisely recall what the plan was. If there are more than two plans illustrated, each would have the abbreviation for the plan delineated. Since both plans were of the increasing premium variety, I called one "Increasing Premium Without Equity" and the other "Increasing Premium With Equity."

I ran the illustration for thirty years. It was at the suggestion of my secretary, Lori, that I started to illustrate the cash value and the total premiums at the top of the page. She pointed out to me it was more shocking to see the zeroes as the first thing as opposed to the last thing at the bottom of the page, which you saw in Illustration 4-1. Lori was right and this is how we do all of our proposals. Thirty-year equity is the cash value and thirty-year premiums is the aggregate for the period demonstrated.

It is obvious to see both total premiums are approximately the same, $8,099-$9,088. But the equities are vastly different, $0-$31,758. Most times there are no questions regarding the comparisons but when the query of "Why" comes, my response is just a matter of time and money. The "With" equity plan requires higher, early money and rises faster but eventually disappears in the 25th year. The "Without" equity plan continues to rise forever. The interview is a fast one when it is displayed in this fashion. I must strongly clarify one thing, though. There is no substitute for selling the need. What I am demonstrating with these simplified illustrations are the solutions and closes. They do not take the place of establishing a common agreement on what the problems and needs are. I vigorously shout to you these illustrations go a long way toward closing cases very easily but don't try shortcuts. You must establish the need.

You can easily determine the two columns illustrated here are the net premium columns of two ledger statements. In previous books I referred to the "cut and paste" method of doing the displays. We now have our IBM PC, *Lotus 1,2,3* program designed to give us just this front sheet

Illustration 5-1

Dale__________________ **Face Amount $100,000**

	Increasing Premium Without Equity	Increasing Premium With Equity
30-Year Equity	**$-0-**	**$31,758**
30-Year Premiums	**8,099**	**9,088**
Year		
1	119	179
2	121	209
3	123	269
4	125	331
5	128	392
6	130	450
7	132	508
8	136	549
9	138	583
10	141	614
11	143	640
12	149	668
13	158	693
14	170	712
15	185	724
16	201	731
17	220	653
18	238	571
19	256	487
20	277	400
21	303	311
22	329	219
23	361	125
24	393	27
25	433	–72
26	475	–174
27	525	–273
28	588	–376
29	658	–479
30	744	–583
	(YRT)	(G-15)

if that is all we want, or the full ledger statements along with it. The machine does all the kerchunking inside and only delivers what we want to see. If all we want is the composite illustration, that is all we ask to have printed.

Illustration 5-2 is very straightforward. It lists two plans: 15-Year Graded Premium and, 20-Year Graded Premium. It was designed for a young woman whom I had never met. She was an attorney who just entered the practice with her sister. I was referred to them by another attorney. I called Jeanne and her sister, Pam, on the phone and they asked that I mail the proposal to them and then follow up with an interview.

I had it made in the amount of $100,000 without even knowing what could be sold. I frequently make up proposals for this amount not knowing what her ultimate need may be. It is easy to do the math either up or down from a starting point of $100,000. Because I was mailing the proposals I used the names of the plans just as they were printed in the rate book. It was easy for the women to determine which plan was the right one for them. The summary at the top showed the input of money and the accumulation of the cash. These figures were very close so the deciding factor would be the ability to pay premiums.

The 15-Year plan started at a lower figure but rose faster. The 20-Year plan started higher but did not rise too far beyond the initial year; it also returned more money in dividends in the later years.

I did follow up with a phone call, met the women and sold them each $100,000 of 20-Year GPL. I also sold a small amount of disability income on the two of them. The total premium came to nearly $2,500, so it was not too bad a case considering it was a call I had initially serviced by mail. The important thing is they are clients of mine and, with proper service, they can become much larger. In any event, I now have two young attorneys who will act as centers of influence.

Just like learning ballroom dancing, you have to start with a simple step and then add to it so, eventually, you can become accomplished and sophisticated. In dancing it is the box step. This becomes the basis for everything that comes later. The flair and verve which so many slick dancers show is merely a small extra movement of the hands or feet while crunching out the box step.

This is not only true in dancing but also in everything in life. At the base of all things there is a simple pattern which repeats itself over and over again. It is also quite true of my simplified proposals. The one you

Illustration 5-2

Jeanne______________	**Face Amount $100,000**	
	15-Year Graded Premium Life	**20-Year Graded Premium Life**
30-Year Equity	**$32,830**	**$34,768**
30 Year Premiums	**9,668**	**7,421**
Year		
1	187	499
2	215	501
3	278	519
4	344	533
5	406	546
6	472	557
7	531	564
8	574	568
9	611	568
10	643	564
11	674	558
12	705	547
13	731	534
14	750	517
15	764	496
16	767	465
17	686	429
18	601	392
19	513	348
20	423	300
21	330	246
22	235	141
23	137	21
24	37	–91
25	–67	–202
26	–168	–312
27	–270	–425
28	–374	–538
29	–480	–654
30	–587	–770
	(G-15)	(G-20)

have just studied as Illustration 5-2 used the names of life insurance plans. I did that because I was sending the forms through the mail before I ever met the prospects. I did not want to get too fancy at a time when I had no control since I would not be present.

Illustration 5-3 is a variation of Illustration 5-2. Mark, who is the client, is also an attorney who was referred by another center of influence. The difference in this interview is the fact that Mark came into the office, so the control was with me. Here I was showing three plans: Yearly Renewable Term; Graded Premium Life-20 and; Graded Premium Life-15 as denoted at the bottom of the columns. I displayed term here because I wanted to show the utter folly to this young man of starting a term program. During the thirty-year period the total premiums amounted to $14,024 with no return of cash; either one of the graded premium policies gave a very decent return.

The unique difference in this illustration is not mentioning the names of the insurance plans. Here, I related the policies to segments of his profession which showed the degree of competency and value of the lawyer. "Law Student" was the lowest form of early cost but a plan which ultimately amounted to nothing; this was term insurance. "Attorney" was 20-GPL which was the best of the three plans. "Paralegal" was a suitable profession but one which did not measure up to "Attorney" in every way and, ultimately, did not earn as much.

Please take note of putting the plan you desire to sell in the center. I point this out once again because people take comfort in the middle and, more frequently than not, choose to concentrate on the middle offering even before I start to discuss the entire proposal. Such was the case in this interview with Mark. He was an attorney and he talked about the "Attorney" plan. Interestingly enough, he did ask me questions about buying term and investing the difference. I responded with a question of my own, "In the first year the difference is $435 (column two, $586 minus column one, $151.) How much can you make investing that kind of difference?"

He bought $200,000 of the "Attorney" plan along with $100,000 for his wife and a $2,500 monthly disability income plan for himself. It did turn out to be a very nice sale and it all started with a visual the client could understand. Mark had many questions and when he left I gave him the full computer ledger statement. He was somewhat of a technical type of person and he liked having the full computer run, in addition to my

Illustration 5-3

Mark____________________ **Face Amount $100,000**

	Law Student	Attorney	Paralegal
30-Year Equity	**$–0–**	**$37,981**	**$36,090**
30-Year Premiums	**14,024**	**10,330**	**13,092**
Year			
1	151	586	221
2	150	598	241
3	150	621	324
4	152	640	406
5	156	658	488
6	164	671	568
7	172	678	633
8	183	687	690
9	194	691	743
10	209	691	789
11	226	685	829
12	246	676	870
13	265	659	901
14	288	638	924
15	310	612	944
16	338	580	953
17	369	544	860
18	401	504	764
19	437	457	665
20	476	406	565
21	519	350	461
22	573	232	352
23	634	104	249
24	708	–12	143
25	798	–131	35
26	903	–251	–74
27	1021	–372	–187
28	1138	–496	–303
29	1271	–623	–421
30	1422	–752	–541
	(YRT-100)	(GPL-20)	(GPL-15)

NOVEMBER 1984

summary sheet. Yet he was not at all offended by the terminology I used. In fact, he told me it gave him a faster start to understanding the kinds of policies he should have been considering.

When I search for the names to put on these illustrations, I sit down and give some thought to the job or product which suits the prospect best. Most times I can come up with the preferred product or the fancier title by myself but if I can't, I resort to allowing the prospect's own office or store helping me. An example of this shows up in the next illustration called "Herb."

Herb owned a fancy meat market. In making his illustration, I wanted to show the difference among term(YRT), whole life(ECL), and graded premium life(G20). I did not know the terminology for the different cuts of meat so I called his market and asked the first voice to answer which were the best, good, and decent choices. She told me prime rib, round steak, and hamburger. I arranged them with the high price cut in the center. Herb's eyes went right to the "Prime Rib" because that is what he likes to sell to his customers. He was magnetically attracted to this column. He wanted to see the differences as to why this one cost more than the other two. He was really preconditioned to opt for the best.

As he did his own studying he noticed the value of the highest return on his savings along with the decreasing premiums sooner than the other plans. Herb was 60-years-old so a $200,000 policy of "Prime Rib" was a nice sale but that is what he wanted after he examined the alternatives. The real object of the form is to get the prospect to give all the options a fair hearing and not make a decision out-of-hand of the lowest cost today. The names I use make the person think and search out why my best product stacks up to his or her best product. Their nomenclature is more familiar to them than ours so why should I teach them a new language as promoted by actuaries and marketing departments. I am my own marketing department and my own advertising agency.

As I lecture around the country I am asked whether or not some of my clients think my designer illustrations are hokey. The answer is no. I have never had a problem using this method of show and tell. To the contrary, I have had problems on occasion explaining why Select Term is different than Yearly Renewable Term to 100, or what the difference is between Econolife and Estate Benefit Life, if they are both whole life policies.

Illustration 5-4

Herb____________		**Face Amount $100,000**	
	Hamburger	**Prime Rib**	**Round Steak**
Equity at 65	**$-0-**	**$ 83,015**	**$47,370**
Premium to Age 65	**52,368**	**82,603**	**72,736**
Year			
1	2760	10648	5820
2	3090	9630	5850
3	3463	8935	5812
4	3105	8278	5804
5	3315	7648	5818
6	3510	7053	5858
7	3658	6480	5907
8	3838	5915	5957
9	4138	4713	5250
10	4595	4175	5252
11	5085	3605	5205
12	5615	3040	5140
13	6198	2485	5066
	(YRT)	(ECL)	(G20)

Illustration 5-5 was made for a young executive who was on the move. The need was for $150,000. As happens all the time, what to show became a problem. It's almost like the *Airport* movies; there is a new one every year. With the new breed of policies, there isn't a new one each year but each day. Competition has become fierce in determining which way to slice the bread; do we make it thin or do we make it thick. We now have the capacity to tailor-make any insurance sandwich for the buyer. The ingredients of the sandwich are protection, premium, and cash value. The TV commercials for one of the hamburger franchises scream at us to "have it your way." And that is exactly what has happened to the former conservative, slow-moving insurance business. We, as agents, are like the countermen in delicatessens just taking orders and making the sandwich delight that our customers want.

In this case, I knew the protection was going to be $150,000 but the variable was going to be the ability to pay. The difference between the

Illustration 5-5

Robert________________ **Face Amount $150,000**

	Increasing Premium	Increasing Premium With Enriched Equity	Increasing Premium With Equity
30-Year Equity	**$-0-**	**$56,972**	**$54,135**
30-Year Premiums	**20,586**	**15,120**	**19,263**
Year			
1	212	867	319
2	210	885	349
3	210	919	474
4	213	948	597
5	219	975	720
6	231	993	840
7	243	1004	937
8	260	1018	1023
9	276	1024	1102
10	299	1024	1171
11	324	1015	1231
12	354	1002	1293
13	383	976	1339
14	417	945	1374
15	450	906	1404
16	492	857	1417
17	539	803	1278
18	587	743	1134
19	641	673	985
20	699	596	835
21	764	513	679
22	845	336	516
23	936	144	361
24	1047	–31	202
25	1182	–209	40
26	1340	–389	–124
27	1517	–517	–293
28	1692	–757	–467
29	1892	–947	–644
30	2118	–1141	–824
	(YRT-100)	(GPL-20)	(GPL-15)

SEPTEMBER 1984

center column(GPL-20) and the last column(GPL-15) was very slight in the 30th-year cash values. However, the early premium increases and the ultimate return of tax-free dividends was greatly in favor of GPL-20.

Robert was a pretty fancy guy who dressed nicely, drove a nice automobile and was learning to live the good life. I wanted to have him make the choice as to which was the best for him in the long run. More importantly, I wanted it to be his idea. Columns two and three are similar in that both have increasing premiums *with* equity, so it might have been a tough job to explain these subtle nuances unless the listener was in a mood to receive small details. My job was to try and find a word which accomplished this. I chose the word "Enriched" and it worked perfectly. His eyes went straight to column two and he wanted to know what the differences were; he *really* wanted to know.

When I explained the modulated effect of grading over twenty years instead of fifteen, and the ongoing, increasing tax-free dividend after the twenty-fourth year, he was immediately willing to purchase the "Enriched" plan. This illustration was not one where I attempted to liken the policies to the occupation of the client but rather to find a word which matched his personality.

The prospect for Illustration 5-6 was Ken, a CPA, who already had a term policy in force with me. I used four columns for this summary. I labeled the first column of his illustration "Existing Insurance" and demonstrated the premiums to age 65, $56,453, and the equity of $0. I then took him through two graded premium plans called "Increasing Premium With Equity" and "Increasing Premium With Enriched Equity." The object of the enriched plan was to show the lower aggregate premium and the higher cash value. The fourth column was called "Universal Life." At the bottom of the columns you will notice I used symbols to outline the plans to me.

I really thought Ken would buy the "Enriched" plan but he fooled me and opted for the UL. It didn't make too much difference since either one was a nice conversion from the term. This has proven to be a great format sheet for making conversions since the term policy does not stack up too well in the long haul. Any one of the other plans looks a lot better when it is demonstrated side by side. I must say again that my purpose is to allow me to show all the features of a plan without the client jumping to a conclusion too quickly based upon previous preconceptions.

Illustration 5-6

Ken__________________ **Face Amount $250,000**

Equity at Age 65	**$-0-**	**$95,983**	**$100,415**	**$207,220**
Premium at Age 65	**56,453**	**54,980**	**44,188**	**52,553**
Year	**Existing Insurance**	**Increasing Premium With Equity**	**Increasing Premium With Enriched Equity**	**Universal Life**
1	405	775	2033	1946
2	430	808	2103	1946
3	465	1100	2177	1946
4	505	1405	2242	1946
5	553	1700	2291	1946
6	600	1985	2324	
7	655	2215	2350	1946
8	710	2430	2363	1946
9	778	2625	2361	1946
10	853	2803	2349	1946
11	930	2958	2323	1946
12	1020	3110	2276	1946
13	1115	3245	2219	1946
14	1220	3355	2152	1946
15	1350	3463	2081	1946
16	1500	3550	1999	1946
17	1683	3238	1902	1946
18	1903	2928	1793	1946
19	2160	2610	1674	1946
20	2450	2280	1534	1946
21	2738	1943	1378	1946
22	3065	1600	1010	1946
23	3435	1258	588	1946
24	3085	910	215	1946
25	3305	570	-150	1946
26	3510	230	-515	1946
27	3658	-110	-880	1946
	(YRT-100)	(GPL-15)	(GPL-20)	(UL)

SEPTEMBER 1984

I don't think I have to do too much explaining regarding the remaining visuals in the rest of the book. It becomes apparent after a while what form the proposals are taking. In Illustration 5-7, Charles is a CPA. Do I need to say more? The illustration was positioned so that the plan I wanted to sell was in the center column. It also had his profession on it. The other two columns represented phases of his industry but not the elite status of a CPA. I truly felt the best policy for him was the GPL-20. My purpose, once again, was to get him to be curious as to why the "CPA" plan was the best. By looking at the title, he liked the idea of choosing the high-priced spread, but now he wanted to discover the fine nuances of the better plan for him.

As is customary for a one interview close, I show the insurance in $100,000 lots. As we talked we determined $200,000 was the proper amount for him and that is what was placed.

I should point out something else about these illustrations. You have probably noticed most of them are dated in the lower right hand corner of the page. I do this for a number of reasons. Chief among them is to have an exact reference point for future meetings. In this one the date is September, 1984. Often, we have to do more than one interview and the figures become more exact for the specific needs. Sometimes we have to show different plans in subsequent meetings. If we don't date them they all start looking alike. Also, it takes away any confusion later on when refreshing our memories, both mine and the clients', as to what was said many years ago.

Just by looking at the center column of Illustration 5-8 (page 76) I am sure you can determine Maury is an optometrist. The column labeled "Optician" is not hard to figure out, but even I had second thoughts about using the one called "Sanford." If you have never seen the TV show *Sanford And Son* you will not know to what I am referring. But if you have see it you will recall Fred Sanford was a junk dealer. He only wore glasses when he had to read a document but he had no spectacles of his own. In a side drawer in a dresser, he had fifteen or twenty pairs which had been collected over the years in trading junk. When he had to read something, he went to the drawer, grabbed a pile of glasses, threw them on the table, and started to put them up to his eyes one by one until he found one out of which he could see fairly well. It was a hilarious scene and always got a big laugh from the audience. To my mind it's the cheapest,

Illustration 5-7

Charles________________		**Face Amount $100,000**	
	Bookkeeper	**CPA**	**Accountant**
30-Year Equity	**$–0–**	**$35,833**	**$33,911**
30-Year Premiums	**11,640**	**9,415**	**12,149**
Year			
1	155	543	205
2	154	550	236
3	151	570	307
4	150	586	379
5	150	603	455
6	152	617	528
7	156	627	592
8	164	632	643
9	172	632	686
10	183	633	729
11	194	630	768
12	209	622	805
13	226	609	835
14	246	593	862
15	265	569	878
16	288	541	889
17	310	507	802
18	338	469	714
19	369	427	622
20	401	379	528
21	437	325	433
22	476	217	334
23	519	92	231
24	573	–22	128
25	634	–134	25
26	708	–247	–77
27	798	–362	–184
28	903	–479	–291
29	1021	–596	–400
30	1138	–718	–513
	(YRT-100)	(GPL-20)	(GPL-15)

SEPTEMBER 1984

Illustration 5-8

Maury________________	**Face Amount $100,000**		
	Optician	**Optometrist**	**"Sanford"**
Equity At 65	**$48,971**	**$51,025**	**$–0–**
Premium To Age 65	**–2,137**	**–5,970**	**22,211**
Year			
1	175	472	161
2	211	471	160
3	271	493	159
4	333	513	157
5	394	529	155
6	453	541	154
7	510	550	151
8	551	554	150
9	587	559	150
10	621	559	152
11	649	555	156
12	678	548	164
13	701	535	172
14	722	524	183
15	740	508	194
16	752	489	209
17	681	463	226
18	610	434	246
19	532	398	265
20	451	356	288
21	369	312	310
22	284	217	338
23	197	107	369
24	107	9	401
25	14	–92	437
26	–81	–197	476
27	–178	–303	519
28	–279	–412	573
29	–376	–519	634
30	–475	–627	708
	(G-15)	(G-20)	(YRT)

July 1984

yet the most costly and inefficient, way to see. Accordingly, I named the term plan "Sanford."

Maury had seen *Sanford and Son* and immediately asked me if the "Sanford" plan referred to the television show. I told him yes. He thought it was "cute" but he got the idea; he bought the "Optometrist" plan.

I am sure by now just looking at the next illustration for Pamela, you can tell the line of work in which she was engaged; she was a computer operator. Pamela also happens to be the wife of Maury (Illustration 5-8) and the interview was done at the same time as his. She understood the reasoning immediately. Even more fortunate was the fact of her working with an IBM system. She told me how good her system was and how different computers had different applications, depending upon type of result desired. I told her the same thing applied to an insurance program. I could have said anything I wanted but Pamela was determined to own "IBM" because that is what she used and for her job it was the most suitable machine.

I should point out in both the Maury and Pamela presentations you see a negative figure for "Premium to Age 65." The reason for this is both of these people were in their early twenties and, by the time they reach 65, there will have been enough dividends paid on the reduction method to exceed the premiums paid. For example, in Illustration for 5-9 for the "Digital" plan, Pamela would receive $5,022 more than she has paid in premiums. Her total gain would have been $53,993, which is the total of cash value $48,971, plus the excess dividends $5,022. This sure makes the "Atari" plan, which is term, look noncompetitive by comparison.

I leave it to you to look at the titles at the top and the codes at the bottom of the columns to figure out what are the plans of insurance. By this time you should be getting adept at the naming of plans. If you have a problem with matching any of them, call me. My name is in the MDRT directory. As I go around the country lecturing, or when I hear by mail or phone from other agents, I am amused at some of the adaptations they are putting on their policies. My daughter, Shelley, is also using this system. She recently told me about one of the interviews she did with the choices being, "Band-Aid Plan," "Cardiologist," and "General Practitioner." I did not have to ask what profession she was interviewing.

What's in a name? A lot if we apply our brains to the process.

Illustration 5-9

Pamela____________________ **Face Amount $100,000**

	Digital	IBM	Atari
Equity At 65	**$48,971**	**$51,025**	**$–0–**
Premium To Age 65	**–5,022**	**–8,214**	**17,076**
Year			
1	165	450	113
2	196	447	117
3	251	467	119
4	308	485	121
5	364	498	123
6	418	508	125
7	470	515	128
8	506	517	130
9	537	519	132
10	566	518	136
11	589	511	138
12	613	502	141
13	631	487	143
14	647	474	149
15	660	455	158
16	667	434	170
17	596	406	185
18	525	375	201
19	447	336	220
20	366	293	238
21	284	246	256
22	199	151	277
23	112	41	303
24	22	57	329
25	–71	–158	361
26	–166	–263	393
27	–263	–369	433
28	–364	–478	475
29	–461	–585	525
30	–560	–693	588
	(G-15)	(G-20)	(YRT)

July 1984

6

Business Ain't Bad

Those of you who have already been engaged in the sale of life insurance for business purposes will be aware of the next little section which outlines the format for selling business insurance. However, the review won't hurt. Those of you who have not been introduced to the business market will find it is a rather easy application of the life insurance "needs" principle.

When I do seminars for insurance companies, or other life underwriter organizations, I first ask if anyone has ever sold a deferred compensation policy. There will always be someone who sells business insurance so I receive an affirmative answer. I ask about the color of the contract and let us assume the answer is grey. I then question if anyone in the same company has ever sold some buy-sell insurance. I again inquire about the color of the policy. Once more, the answer is grey. I ask if anyone has sold retirement insurance. Here, too, the policy is grey. Key employee? Grey. Creditor policy? Grey. Split dollar on the business owner? Again, grey.

What's all this talk about grey when all these business needs are for different purposes? The answer becomes obvious; the policy doesn't change. It is still life insurance issued by the same company in the same color as all their other policies. It is the need which is different and the applicability of the contract toward the solution of the problem. Like all of our interviews, once the problem is fully and genuinely understood, the solution is almost self-evident.

Uncovering and exposing the problem is where the real business insurance skills lie. The emphasis for the new agent in the advanced market should be toward the study of business, retirement, and estate problems. The best courses usually start in the agencies with the supervisors, managers, or other specialists. Later on one should consider LUTC, CLU, ChFC, and other organized study formats. Then it is time to hit the bricks, get your nose bloodied and learn in front of a real live prospect. Do not overlook the value of joint work with an established producer in the area you are entering. If a rookie agent can uncover a qualified prospect for a veteran closer, it is worth a commission split and both parties will come out as winners. The new agent will learn something while earning a comparatively larger commission. The experienced agent will have an easier time making appointments because that is being done by someone else. Also, the rookie agent should do all of the medical and follow-up work. It is know as "on the job training" and, in this fashion, he or she learns more. The veteran agent also gains a great deal of satisfaction by knowing and seeing that a bit of education is being passed on to someone who will benefit. There is a high calling to one who will teach and share; he or she gets more than they give. If you have any doubt about the theory of giving and receiving, try this experiment. It won't cost anything and the chance to gain something is tremendous.

Do something nice for someone; go out of your way to make an investment in kindness. Invest some effort in a fellow human being without expecting a return then stand back because you will be rewarded out of all proportion to your input. One of the greatest rewards is the total feeling of self-satisfaction that wells-up within ourselves when we know we have done a good thing. This relaxing feeling of well-being far surpasses the sense of euphoria sought by the distance runners and the practitioners of meditation. When my daughters were taking their first baby sitting jobs, I would tell them as they left the house, "Give 'em something extra." They did and they are all winners today and have a tenacious attitude toward hard work and the success it brings.

In this book I am not teaching how to enter the business insurance market. Rather, I am concentrating on making the proposals understandable, meaningful, simple, and effective. It is like going to a very fine business or finance school or majoring in business administration in college. They can tell you everything you have to know about doing business except how to generate it yourself. This is especially so in the insurance business where we must originate the business ourselves. In order to succeed in our field one must be an absolute self-starter. That is my assumption here because if you don't have the will to succeed in your computer, which is your stomach, or in your brain, neither I nor anyone else can help you. The seed may be there but only one person in the world can be assured of it—you!!

It's ironic that my purpose is to try and cut down the computer ledger monsters while, at the same time, we have people within the companies who are like kids at Christmas time after having discovered a new toy. They keep flexing their brains showing all the magic stuff the machines can do.

I remember a few years ago when all we had was a rate book. The computer was a mysterious thing off somewhere in the home office where it was kept in a locked room where one needed the combination, a password, a photograph, and a fingerprint to enter. No smoking, breathing, bad language, or temperature variations were allowed. Then the home offices made all their mistakes in private. Now we all have easy access to a mini-computer and we can make our own mistakes. Somehow, a proposal is never just one; either the waiver of premium is forgotten or the smoking status is cloudy, or someone forgot to use age nearest birthday. You might even get four proposals for just one request for a simple policy.

I don't want this to sound like ancient history but my analogy will show you there is nothing new in the world and history does repeat itself. It used to be we had such things as rate books. They told us the rate per thousand, the guaranteed value at all years for the first twenty, sample values for various ages such as 55, 60, 65, and maybe 70, and certain other items such as waiver of premium and other riders on a per thousand basis. When we quoted a rate, we first found the right age and multiplied it by the amount of insurance desired. We only quoted the rate per year and the total cash values for the periods desired; the proposals were short and sweet.

The computer allowed all the variations to be easily shown. The programmers took over in the marketing departments and this, coupled with the high interest rates of the late 1970's and the early 1980's, plus the changing philosophy of insurance as investment and investments as insurance, (as in universal life) made for the age of disclosure. We are currently having a revolution of deregulation in the insurance industry, in addition to the other signs of the times. Certain regulatory bodies are asking for more disclosure in our presentations to the public. I don't know how much more they can take. We can now show them everything the actuary has to know to design a policy and have it in five minutes, if our computer is not already in use. Dividend applications and minimum deposit combinations are endless. I think we are going a little number happy and trying to let the logic of the figures sell the policies. Unfortunately, the more we show the more there is to see and the more questions and possibilities that come to mind. Then we get asked for more proposals because it is interesting and intriguing to see how this product works. Too often, as a result of overindulgence of paper, no decision is made or a "no" decision is made. My idea is to highlight the important stuff and verbalize everything else, as needed.

Let me tie these two items of the supposed mystery of business insurance and the fascination with larger and more elaborate proposals together. After that I will share some proposals I use for business situations which, hopefully, will untie the knots of mystery. As I mentioned before, business insurance is not an uncharted world; there are methods of learning. If you are interested in the field, your assignment is to do whatever is necessary to go as far as your desires. Remember this phrase, "What can be done by man, can be done by Meisel." Now, just substitute your name for "Meisel." It should now read, "What can be done by man, can be done by *me.* Obviously, business insurance is tougher to do. There is specialized knowledge to be studied but the rewards, financially and in satisfaction, are the compensatory ingredients. If you want it, jump in.

Concerning the area of what to present to the business client to demonstrate his or her needs and solutions, my system is exactly the same as I have shown you regarding individual policies. For a more detailed explanation of matching solutions to problems, refer to *NO, I CAN'T AFFORD IT* also published by The National Underwriter Company.

M.K. was a builder in the Michigan area. His specialty was custom homes although his projects were varied and included some tract homes in subdivisions, condominiums, and apartments. I was introduced to the case through his attorney who had done some estate planning for him and was drawing up all the proper documents to put his house in order. There was a need for $750,000 of liquidity for income for the family. There was considerable wealth and it was to be assumed M.K. would predecease his wife. There would be a sizeable estate but the problems were twofold: first, the matter of everything being tied up in real estate and; secondly, the highly illiquid and volatile value structure of those types of assets.

The attorney and I met prior to the time we would be meeting with the client. I gathered all the information I could regarding the family and business of M.K. In the past he was a term insurance buyer since he felt his real estate ventures were pretty good cash accumulation vehicles. The lawyer's impression was to have an irrevocable trust for this needed $750,000 of insurance. I agreed with this idea and we arranged the meeting.

Present were the client and his wife, the attorney, and the CPA whom I had never met before. I spent about ten hours in my office prior to the meeting preparing Illustration 6-1. For the interview at the client's office, I took my overhead projector, which I always use if there are more than two people at a meeting, otherwise the paper shuffle gets too confusing for me, let alone them. I set up the projector and was about to start talking when the CPA asked, "Is this term?" My response was, "Yes, and I call it "Apartment Rental." We were now right into the middle of the interview.

Please notice all the terms I used for the names of the plans had to do with the construction business. "Apartment Rental" was term as outlined in parentheses at the bottom of the column. I explained that, just like renting an apartment, the rent starts out low at $1,860 and rises to $12,893 in the 24th year when the client would be age 65. Just like any apartment rental there is no equity created. The total rent paid is represented by the "24-Year Premium" as $151,297. No one thought the analogy was hokey and they understood my point immediately.

Column two was called "Mobile Home" and, as is the case with these types of investments, one would usually get back less than the total payments made. This was demonstrated as "24-Year Premium" of $129,783 and "24-Year Equity" of $115,285. The payments were fairly constant, starting at $7,883 (which represented a small extra down payment) and then leveled to $5,300 per year. At the bottom of the column you will see this is a Universal Life plan and at the top you will see I illustrated it at 10.5% interest. The column called "(Value)" showed a varying amount which was the growth of the plan because of the corridor requirement of TEFRA.

Column three was called "Custom Designed" which is a whole life plan from Connecticut Mutual with the name Econolife (Eco). I presented it on a vanishing premium basis of $15,348 for eight years. The total premiums paid in the 24 years is the total which was paid in the first eight, $122,784. Just as any custom home should increase in value, the "24-Year Equity" is $373,034. They liked this plan very much and it had the most questions by all parties. It seemed the client and his wife were used to the highs and lows of income in the building business and they

Illustration 6-1

M. K. **Face Amount $750,000**

24-Year Equity		**$ –0–**	**$115,285**		**$373,034**		**$608,188**		**$285,383**
24-Year Premium		**151,297**	**129,783(10.5%)**		**122,784**		**240,000(10.5%)**		**179,859**

Year	Apartment Rental	Mobile Home	(Value)	Custom Designed	(Value)	Equity Plus Condo	(Value)	Tract Home
1	1860	7883	756156	15348	750000	10000	758460	7855
2	2018	5300	759921	15348	753615	10000	767592	8053
3	2220	5300	763915	15348	759760	10000	777545	8274
4	2408	5300	768062	15348	768492	10000	788308	8464
5	2603	5300	772461	15348	779869	10000	800051	8632
6	2828	5300	777031	15348	794011	10000	812776	8763
7	3098	5300	781768	15348	811003	10000	826565	8856
8	3398	5300	786768	15348	831002	10000	841616	8896
9	3773	5300	791919	0	816405	10000	857925	8914
10	4200	5300	797297	0	803447	10000	875691	8917

11	4725	5300	802689	0	792199	10000	894835	8883
12	5363	5300	808140	0	782611	10000	915555	8811
13	6105	5300	813575	0	774767	10000	937941	8701
14	6945	5300	818847	0	768522	10000	962032	8554
15	7778	5300	824000	0	764166	10000	988078	8340
16	8723	5300	829070	0	761551	10000	1016344	8073
17	9803	5300	833993	0	760833	10000	1047018	7776
18	8715	5300	840003	0	761880	10000	1081618	7419
19	9330	5300	845789	0	764828	10000	1119145	7039
20	9893	5300	851207	0	769819	10000	1159801	6660
21	10283	5300	856073	0	776707	10000	1203789	6243
22	10755	5300	860188	0	785704	10000	1251338	5005
23	11588	5300	863332	0	797878	10000	1302701	1983
24	12893	5300	865285	0	812315	10000	1358188	753
	(YRT-100)	(UL)		(Eco)		(UL)		(GPL-20)

January 1984

liked the idea of making contributions into the trust for only eight years and then not having to be concerned.

The next set of figures was labeled "Equity Plus Condo" and represented Universal Life-Option Two, which is definitely the face amount plus the equity. I showed a level premium of $10,000 resulting in "24-Year Premium" of $240,000 and equity of $608,188, assuming the same 10.5%. You can check the growth of the "(value)" column and see that it is the total of $750,000 and the equity of the policy. They liked this plan, too.

The last column was GPL-20 representing a "Tract Home" which will usually increase in value over the years. In 24 years, premiums of $179,859 will be paid and there would bc an equity value of $285,383. The premium starts at $7,855 and never gets too much higher than that.

My goal in offering these five plans was to be able to discuss the various types of policies in terms they would understand. I had never met them before so I really didn't know much about what to expect, even though the attorney had given me a good background. He did say he thought his client was a term buyer, which turned out to be wrong, and I dreamed a little about how much premium I felt they could afford. Obviously, the term was the lowest early premium for this amount of insurance and the whole life was the highest level premium. In between I went for graded premium life and two flavors of Universal Life. The discussion was serious and meaningful; everyone understood my titles and the chosen plan was the "Custom Designed."

What we had there was a business and estate planning case which was discussed thoroughly in advance by the attorney and the life underwriter, brainstormed by the agent so it made sense for the situation, and presented in an atmosphere conversant to everyone so the solution could be in terms familiar to all. In this way, not too much time was taken explaining all those ledger statements I had in my case. Incidentally, the CPA did ultimately ask me for a full copy of the ledger statement so he could understand all the numbers. I think this was exactly the proper sequence of what should have happened with them.

I mentioned previously we have these discs from the insurance companies programmed in our computer and we run these illustrations on the *Lotus 1,2,3* program. I do not know if any of you have access to these devices but, if you do have the availability of computer illustrations, you can accomplish the same results as I using the "cut and paste" method. What should be done is run the computer ledgers, make a photocopy of the net premium column you are going to show, cut it out, paste up the proposal in the fashion in which you will be using it, and make clear photocopies for your interview.

I spoke earlier of various methods of getting into the business insurance field but I now caution you that if you are not in that phase of development, go slowly. The ideas which I am showing you are used for closing cases after the need has been developed and exposed. No one should change his or her method of operation overnight. If you are engaged in a family and personal insurance practice and it is successful for you, you are a natural candidate to step into the business field. If your clientele is numerous, you have a great natural starting point for prospecting. Everyone of your existing clients either works for themselves or someone else. If they are self-employed, it is easy to make a business approach to someone you already know. If they work for someone else, you are in a position to find out the fringe benefit package of their employer. Also, you can learn a lot about the corporate makeup of the company just by asking people who are already friendly with you.

Along with the other methods of study I previously mentioned for starting in the business market, you also have access to some of the greatest producers in the world who, in effect, will do a "joint" interview with you. I am referring to the proceedings of The Million Dollar Round Table. If you are a member, you are familiar with the book. If not, let me explain how you can share ideas on business insurance and every other advanced underwriting subject with the greatest brains in the industry. If you are not a member, you should have associates or friends who are. Ask to borrow their book of proceedings. Maybe, if you are not a member of the MDRT, the exposure to reading the proceedings of past meetings will help you raise yourself to MDRT production. I save all of my books, which are published each Fall after the June meeting, and try to read the speeches from all the speakers. Some of them I will have seen at the meeting; those which I could not attend, I read.

Very often, I find it helpful to be able to research past proceedings and find out what some of the masters have said regarding cases like the one on which I may be working. I couldn't have better teachers than the ones who have made a science out of the very thing I wish to brainstorm. This, in conjunction with the methods of business training your company offers, along with all the experience you will acquire on the street by striking out on your first few interviews, will give you a tremendous launch into this new and profitable field.

One of the illustrations you will find in the proceedings from the 1982 and 1984 speeches I made at the annual MDRT meeting is entitled, "Methods of Transferring a Business Interest at Death." That illustration outlines the fact that there are only two ways in the whole world on how to conduct any kind of business; wholesale and retail. Our product, combined with a proper business agreement, will accomplish the transaction which we call a buy-sell agreement, on a wholesale basis. Any other method which a client can mention is retail. For a quick understanding of the items for consideration in conducting a buy-sell interview, refer to Illustration 2-1 on page 20.

The shareholders for Illustrations 6-2 and 6-3 were named Hal and Stan and they were in the machinery manufacture business. Both owned fifty percent of the business and they operated as a corporation. They had no formal agreement between them although it was assumed they would buy each other's shares at the death of one of them. Also, there was no funding. A classic case of retail.

In the wholesale-retail interview, I only use one figure to represent the premium for life insurance. I use no ledger statements or any other displays; just one number. In this case, I had done an interview with them on July 10, 1984 and was not successful in closing a sale. They wanted to think it over and see more numbers representing what their cash interest would be twenty years in the future if neither one had died and the insurance was still in force. These second illustrations, dated at the lower right corner, were made to fulfill their request.

I will refer to Illustration 6-2 only to explain the method of presentation; Illustration 6-3 is designed to do exactly as Illustration 6-2. The shareholder in 6-2 is Stan and in 6-3 it is Hal. Their valuation for the business was $500,000 so each interest is $250,000 and that is what is illustrated. Both men were in their mid-fifties.

In column one, I showed Yearly Renewable Term to 100; you can tell this from my code at the bottom. I showed this just to get a basis for what the raw protection would cost. I explained to them this provided coverage on the cheapest, earliest basis available. I called this plan, "INCREASING PREMIUM NO EQUITY." It was important for me to emphasize the point of no equity since the foundation of this interview was to try to create some cash for a possible living buy out in about twenty years. Incidentally, this makes a point upon which we should reflect; it is economically bizarre to buy term insurance to fund a buy-sell deal.

Illustration 6-2

Stan__________________ Face Amount $250,000

20-Year Equity	**$–0–**	**$282,012**	**$532,132**	**$105,642**
20-Year Premiums	**110,540**	**120,153**	**172,460**	**114,081**
Year	**Increasing Premium No Equity**	**Increasing Premium With Equity Flexible**	**Level Premium Same As Shown July 10, 1984**	**Increasing Premium With Equity (Down Payment)**
1	2470	6008	8623	6008
2	2760	6008	8623	2760
3	3090	6008	8623	3090
4	3455	6008	8623	3455
5	3095	6008	8623	3095
6	3305	6008	8623	3305
7	3510	6008	8623	3510
8	3658	6008	8623	3658
9	3838	6008	8623	3838
10	4138	6008	8623	4138
11	4595	6008	8623	4595
12	5085	6008	8623	5085
13	5615	6008	8623	5615
14	6198	6008	8623	6198
15	6868	6008	8623	6868
16	7645	6008	8623	7645
17	8603	6008	8623	8603
18	9670	6008	8623	9670
19	10820	6008	8623	10820
20	12125	6008	8623	12125
	(YRT-100)	(UL-11.5 MIN)	(UL-11.5)	(UL-11.5)

October 1984

Eventually, the term either goes out of existence or out of sight in cost. What sense could that possibly make for funding a deal for a long period of time, especially one which has the hope of some lump sum fund one day in the future? There aren't any better, surer ways of doing this other than the double duty dollars of permanent life insurance. So, my purpose with column one was to establish a foundation, albeit, a weak one. Notice the numbers; with the term they pay $110,540 and recover zero during the twenty-year period.

Column two is called "Increasing Premium With Equity Flexible." From the code at the bottom, you will see this is Universal Life using the current interest rate of 11.5%. You will also notice the phrase "MIN" in the code. This relates to the first annual premium under column four which I will explain shortly. The total premiums are $120,153 and the projected equity is $282,012. At this point, I explained the flexibility and growth potential of the Universal Life concept.

The premium I selected was $6,008. My reasoning was to try to establish around $250,000 of cash value after twenty years.

Column three indicated "Level Premium Same As Shown July 10, 1984." This was the premium I indicated to them in the earlier interview and the one which caused the delay. On that interview, I only expressed the cost of funding the buy-sell contract at "about 7% or 8%." This is the way I do the interview under the "wholesale-retail" format. My purpose was to show them the result of paying a premium of $8,623 throughout and the resulting equity, with a partial eye to a sizable deferred compensation accumulation. After the interview of July 10, 1984, I really felt they could not afford the 7% or 8%. This, too, was a Universal Life plan.

Column four is called "Increasing Premium With Equity (Down Payment)." You will notice the only year which requires a high early premium is year one. In that year the premium is $6,008 which exactly corresponds with the level premium in column two. Thereafter, premiums follow precisely the premiums of the term policy in column one. This is also a Universal Life policy. I called it a "down payment" plan because I was trying to convey to them the flexibility of Universal Life in any way they chose. I explained that if they made the down payment in column four, they could pay any amount they chose as long as they stuck to a minimum of what was in column one. In other words, this was a "do it yourself" buy out plan.

Illustration 6-3

Hal____________ Face Amount $250,000

20-Year Equity	**$–0–**	**$255,910**	**$401,130**	**$136,717**
20-Year Premiums	**136,413**	**127,551**	**154,960**	**139,831**
Year	**Increasing Premium No Equity**	**Increasing Premium With Equity Flexible**	**Level Premium Same As Shown July 10, 1984**	**Increasing Premium With Equity (Down Payment)**
1	2965	6378	7748	6378
2	3283	6378	7748	3283
3	3643	6378	7748	3643
4	4005	6378	7748	4005
5	4433	6378	7748	4433
6	4915	6378	7748	4915
7	4678	6378	7748	4678
8	5010	6378	7748	5010
9	5315	6378	7748	5315
10	5560	6378	7748	5560
11	5830	6378	7748	5830
12	6228	6378	7748	6228
13	6898	6378	7748	6898
14	7650	6378	7748	7650
15	8493	6378	7748	8493
16	9413	6378	7748	9413
17	10408	6378	7748	10408
18	11458	6378	7748	11458
19	12548	6378	7748	12548
20	13685	6378	7748	13685
	(YRT-100)	(UL-11.5 MIN)	(UL-11.5)	(UL-11.5)

October 1984

Hal's comment was, "How can we go wrong by choosing the down payment plan. We can change it year by year, if we have to." Column four eventually was the plan for which we applied for both of them.

The discussion was for business purposes but the display of the plans was really just a numbers exercise once the problem was agreed upon. We established early that an equity was needed later and protection was needed now. The exposition gave them all kinds of options. Paying a difference of $3,538 ($6,008–$2,470) in the first year of the down payment plan created an equity of $105,642 in twenty years. It is tough to say no to a proposal like this once the problem has been exposed.

I don't know what premium they will pay in the second year but I suspect they will continue to pay $6,008. Using the same words as when I explained the illustration to Stan and Hal, "It's a do it yourself insurance plan. As long as you pay the minimum, you can pay anything over that and create some money for living purposes." That is exactly what Universal Life is.

The construction of a sheet like this takes considerable thought concerning the entire problem so the visual can be made to reflect the needs. In this case, I felt the words "down-payment" had some validity considering they were in a business which required them to make down payments when they purchased something. The idea of a larger dump in premium during the first year of the Universal Life and then following the term schedule seemed to fit perfectly and, as shown by the applications I received, it did. It is necessary to do the brainstorming in the office for a longer period of time so that the time spent in the interview is pinpointed and brief. Hopefully, these formats start the flow of ideas for you so you can construct profitable ones of your own. At least you have a matrix to follow if you start with some of the ones I have reprinted here.

The Robotics Tank Company was owned equally by three brothers and it operated as a corporation. The brothers were named Thomas, David, and Brian. The products they manufactured were underground tanks of all sizes and barrels of all sizes. I met with Thomas for the purpose of discussing how to bring the buy-sell agreement up-to-date with the current value of the business. We had done business in 1981 by initiating the first insurance in their stock redemption planning. We had performed various other types of business and personal insurance for them during the interim.

Illustration 6-4

Robotics Tank Company

$200,000 for Thomas, David & Brian **Face Amount $600,000**

	Fiberglass	Steel
20-Year Equity	**$–0–**	**$186,656**
20-Year Premiums	**130,578**	**162,092**
Year		
1	2430	7961
2	2670	8074
3	2944	8224
4	3270	8381
5	3660	8525
6	4114	8650
7	4632	8751
8	5180	8815
9	5766	8850
10	6442	8844
11	6590	8821
12	6644	8766
13	7176	8682
14	7682	8589
15	8196	8459
16	8832	7744
17	9724	6988
18	10804	6694
19	11364	6331
20	12458	5943
	(YRT)	(G-20)

November 1984

The interview which I gave in 1981 was the "Wholesale-Retail" presentation. It worked to convey the need and solution but I had to present extensive figures to make the sale to the shareholders. It was not an easy one in spite of the initial interest. It took a number of meetings but, ultimately, resulted in a $25,000 premium case.

My purpose on the most recent interview was to stimulate interest in fully funding the agreement. Business had not been good for them since 1981 but the values had grown because of land acquisitions and other equipment growth. Tom told me to send him some figures to increase the coverage on each stockholder by $200,000. I remembered my previous interview which had an awful lot of paper for me because I was transmitting the ideas and premiums for three separate shareholders. These were not easy guys to convince. I decided to use the two column "name" interview. You will find this represented by Illustration 6-4.

I did not have to ask anyone which product was the stellar seller; I knew the best in the industry was a steel tank. I also knew from years of talking with these people the generic product was fiberglass. Our computer is programmed to make these two or more column visuals. It is also programmed to make composite illustrations showing one or more lives as one total cost for the corporation. However, it is not as yet programmed to do both of these things, although it could be done if we wanted to take the time and expense to do it.

What we did was run the computer for the composite illustration for the three ages as a total. We did this for term and the Graded Premium-20. Then we had the net premium columns typed into the two appropriate columns. After the computer did the calculations, it was not too much of a job to have a secretary do the typing. If you look at the whole sheet, you will see this task should not have taken more than fifteen minutes. That's about as tough as the work gets in our preparation system.

The "Fiberglass" column, which is term, requires a premium of $2,430 in the first year, and $12,458 in the twentieth year. This totals $130,578 in premiums and grosses an equity of zero. The "Steel" plan requires total premiums of $162,092 but it creates cash values of $186,656. I sent the sheet ahead as they had asked me to do. When I called for the appointment Tom said to me, "I don't know about this 'Steel' and 'Fiberglass' deal." In a backhanded way he was paying me a compliment. He was not being snide but was telling me he was on the same wave length as I was, immediately.

When I did the interview, all the shareholders agreed readily that "Steel" was the best plan for their needs. They told me it was durable because it held its value and, even though it started at a higher cost, maintenance in the future years would keep the annual upkeep almost level. During the same period the other product would be increasing all the time and eventually would need replacing. They said it better than I could have so I kept relatively silent during the entire closing interview.

As we have gone through these illustrations I have tried to share with you my procedures for determining the kinds of products sold or the businesses operated by the clients. I have outlined my code at the bottom of the columns to show which plans of insurance I have used. I have also demonstrated why it is most advantageous to place the policy you wish to sell in the center column. Let's just say the following is the test part of the text.

Answer the following questions:

1. What are the plans of insurance you can use in your proposals?
2. What kind of business does your client own?
3. What column, and why, is the prospect more likely to choose?

If you have trouble with any of the questions, call me. We'll do some personal telephone counseling.

Conclusion

Selling business insurance can be tough or it can he hard. The choice is strictly up to the agent; it has nothing whatever to do with the prospect. A business person has more of a regard for his or her business assets than he or she has for personal assets. They know from whence the source of everything springs. They can see the logic of protecting and placing a funded value on this income producing wellspring. We can make it a lot easier for them by setting out the problems and solutions in terms they can understand and with which they can identify, as opposed to our own jargon which is as much a mystery to them as the backroom stuff or their ventures are to us. Study and prepare but don't try to overwhelm the prospect with big words just because you want him or her to write a big check.

I'll close this chapter with a funny story one of my client's told me. He has been a client nearly as long as I have been selling insurance, which was in 1956. I visited his home twenty-five years ago when his son was born. Now the boy is in business with his dad and the father is having mixed feelings about this intruder who is doing such a fine job. He is proud of his son but he feels a pang when longtime customers call on the phone and ask for Steve instead of Larry.

We have discussed business continuation insurance for the past year or so and dad has told me he is interested. But he is not quite sure about how he wants to arrange all of his affairs with regard to this young lad, with him having the business and his mother having all the cash. Larry is having trouble letting go. I suppose he feels that when it is written down and funded, just like the Bible, *it is written.*

We will be doing the work soon but as yet there has been nothing concrete done. Steve takes an aggressive stance to all of this delay. He knows, someday, all of this will be his, on one basis or another. He enjoys the business meetings we have and he enjoys his father's muted joy at seeing the business grow and multiply while he is taking a very active hand in the day-to-day activities. The son has said to the father that no matter what is done, he is ready. There are only two phone numbers he carries in his wallet: one is the lawyer's and; the other is the sign painter's. Destiny is in his corner.

Our job is to do it wholesale.

This completes Chapter Six. If we do our jobs well, it keeps our clients and their heirs away from Chapters Seven and Eleven.

7

Price May Vary. . .

There was a time when one could pick up a rate book and in an instant determine a rate. There was only one rate per age, and the only distinction was the gender of the buyer. Smoking was not a factor in the rate. Actually, it was a factor but everyone shared the cost. There was no distinction between smokers and non-smokers. We only had two or three plans which we sold. Although it was not as blunt as, "Take it or leave it," once the rate was related to the prospect the job became one of salesmanship on the basis of need and the ability of the salesperson. All the efforts were concentrated on the problem at hand and not whether or not the rate could be tailored. Of course, there were the times when a recalculation had to be made from permanent to term or some other idea. But, usually, the sale was made in the mind of the agent after giving full consideration to the needs and problems of the client. The escalation or descension of the premium was of only casual interest. The cash value at age 65 was the major thing; people wanted that. I can also recall a time when the settlement options stacked up favorably with the monthly income one could derive from a bank account and we focused heavily on the guaranteed nature of the insured income options.

The proposals were simple, if you used one. Most often, I did not. The forms were preprinted, one sheet illustrations which had boxes for the first years premium, fifth year, tenth year, twentieth year, and age 65. The cash value followed the same outlined years. If you wanted something else you had to be inventive to get it in. There was no such thing as showing every year's cash value, dividend, and other factors from present age to some far away point in the future. The problem of need was uppermost and once we determined the ability to pay, we did not make a further problem out of variable premium rates.

Times changed. Interest rates rose. Mortality improved. Competition heightened. The stock market started to sell insurance. The surgeon general made a damning report on smoking. Term became popular; permanent did not. Graded premium came into prominence. Dividend scales soared. Universal Life emerged. Computers reigned. Company advertising got nasty. Commissions got cut; expenses escalated. Congress changed the taxation laws for both stock and mutual companies.

The home offices were telling us these were the best of times. The atmosphere in the marketplace was telling us these were the worst of times.

We, as agents, started to get shell-shocked. We could not keep up with the changing scene. The plans and rates changed so fast it was impossible to persist with one parent company, let alone represent a clientele by knowing what was available in the full marketplace. Term rate cards and advertisements were in our mail everyday. The rate kept dropping. Each agent thought he or she had found the fountain of youth; each had just heard about another drop in premiums. It got to the point where I was asking clients who told me they just heard about another plan cheaper than the one I was showing, "Was that Monday's term or Tuesday's term?"

Universal came into its own. Now there was no such thing as a rate book; just push the buttons and stand back. The clients took the cues we were giving them and asked for just one more proposal. The standard objection became, "Run me another proposal." We further added to the confusion by doing it. This led the clients to doubt whether they were getting the full story; it seemed there was always a way of getting it cheaper. We salespeople became product pushers. Since the numbers were so easy to get we got them and, just like the phone company which says to let your fingers do the walking, we tried to let the figures do the selling for us. It still goes on and I suppose it will for a long time or as long as we have computer capacity.

I saw Illustration 7-1 in a friend's office. He could not remember where he got it so I guess we will have to say it's anonymous. It tells the story of today's selling climate very well. We are able to fine tune a plan to exactly where the prospect wants to see it. If the attitude is more toward savings, we can do that. If it is more toward protection, we can accomplish that, too. We have two ways to do it. Either the company has a plan which is right on target or we will run the computer to create a policy right in front of the prospect's eyes. There are those agents who make a very fine show of having the prospect come into their office and look over their shoulder while they feed into the computer the information as the client dictates it. It is then tough to say "no" to a plan which does

Illustration 7-1

exactly what the author of the idea wanted. There is also that mystique of seeing your own "Frankenstein" come to life; It's known as the "hands on" method.

So, indeed, the price may vary due to the attitude of the customer. This is great but the first attitude of a wary buyer expressed to the agent is not necessarily the true one. Our job is to do a good job of fact finding and suit the product to the fact situation. I do change the price according to the attitude of the customer, but my purpose is to show them exactly what they have asked for in the simplest fashion to understand.

Before we look at the next few illustrations let us talk about the idea of varying the mind of the prospect according to the attitude of the agent. An old life insurance maxim says the sale is made in the mind of the agent. This is absolutely true; we can do what we believe we can do.

It is tough to live with all the rejection we receive as salespeople. It is tough to get names, then it is tough to process those names until we get appointments. It is tough to make sales and it is tough to get the policies issued. Then we must keep those policies in force. We sometimes wonder to ourselves why no one likes us; there are stumbling blocks every step of the way. Yet just as the sale is made in the mind of the agent, so are the problems made in the mind of the agent. It is simple to figure out how many calls it takes to make an appointment and it is easy to figure out how many appointments it takes to make a sale. All of our activities are strictly a numbers game; everything in our profession is a matter of the law of averages. If we believe that, we are in control of all of our endeavors. Each thing we do is a matter of the approach which we give to it. With careful thought we can improve on all phases of our operations.

We sometimes make excuses for our prospects and clients before they make them for themselves. Apparently, we sometimes put pictures in our minds of how we want things to be or how we perceive our prospects want them to be; many times we are wrong. We have to make decisions at times in our careers on what kind of market we are going to approach, what kind of studies we are going to pursue, and what kind of business practice we want to attain for the long run. We can do whatever we want to do.

The problems, most of the time, are in our own minds. Let's take the example of getting people to come to our offices, as opposed to going to them for appointments. My associate, Donald R. Haas, made this transition by asking one question, "When can you come in?" Having said it, there was no more thinking to do; it was out in the open and it became a final alternative regarding the time. If the client truly can't come in, some other accommodation will be made. However, most of the time they can come in.

One of the decisions I made years ago was to work in the business market and stay out of the personal market. That's not to say I have not written personal insurance in the last few years, because I have many times written small policies for friends or relatives or their friends or relatives. My brother, Chuck, who is in the trucking business, called me with a prospect who was the chief buyer for a large Detroit automotive supply company. The situation was that the man's brother-in-law had died recently and the man was concerned about his own estate planning insurance. Chuck gave me a very good reference, called me and said that I should call on Dick—which I did. I asked Dick when he could come into the office and he told me that would be impossible. He wanted his wife along but they have kids involved with little league and other activities and it just could not be done. So I made an evening appointment for 7:00 p.m. on the opposite side of Detroit from where I live, and went to the man's house.

Although he was the chief buyer, the company was in an austerity program because of the 1983 economic situation in Detroit and, consequently his salary had been cut. He owned about $35,000 of personal insurance, consisting of $15,000 of Whole Life (some of it in family policies) and $20,000 of term riders. The company had a $55,000 group insurance policy on him. We did a simple written/verbal programming plan and there was a need for another $40,000 of insurance. We talked about the difference between term insurance and whole life insurance, and we settled upon a twenty-year graded premium life policy. I wrote the application and accepted a check for the conditional receipt. In the end, the interview took about two and one-half hours and by the time I got home it was 10:30 p.m.

I had started the day at 7:00 a.m. with an office appointment and I was really tired. But I was happy because I had helped a small, middle-income family achieve what they wanted to do, especially since the message of loss of income had been driven home to them because of the death of the brother-in-law. I really felt good about the whole transaction.

The next morning the wife called me and said they still wanted to think about the transaction and she was going to call in a couple of other insurance agents over the weekend. She said she would like to stop by and pick up their policies, which I had taken for a policy audit, and their check.

Dick's wife had stated her case very well on the telephone and I did not object. She said she wanted to think it over, and I was prepared to do exactly what she wanted. I told her I would send the policies through the mail along with the check, but she insisted on coming to my office that day and picking up the material. This she did.

The point of this story is that, although they could not find the time previously to come to my office to talk about the insurance, when it was a matter of picking up a $40 check, it became imperative to spend $10 of gas driving to get it, along with an hour and one-half round trip. In other words, if the mission is meaningful people can find a reason to come to you. It is important to realize: one, that people will do what you ask them to do and; two, you must give them sufficient reason to make them do it.

Continuing along the lines of the variance of price and the law of large numbers, consider Illustration 7-2 as an example of selling what the client wants, but also making the sale. It is nice to diagnose a case perfectly and sell exactly what we think is the best product for the need. However, what we want to sell makes absolutely no difference if it is not what the client truly desires. We may have our justification why one plan is better than another for a particular fact situation, but the client may have his or her own reasons which are precisely valid in their mind. It is our job only to teach and guide up to a certain point. Once all the facts are presented, the choice is that of the buyer. They will have their own ideas for preferring a certain policy over another. That reason may be silly or it may be serious; it may be as simple as not being able to afford the desired plan and not wanting to say so. It may be a function of not wanting to pay the higher dollars now even though they could afford it.

At a certain point, ours is not to reason why; just take the order because now the prime job is to gain a client. The convincing, teaching and selling can come later. Illustration 7-2 was just such an interview. The need for Art R. was $2,000,000 for keyman insurance on his own life for the benefit of his corporation. He told me he wanted the cheapest insurance I could find. I didn't know if this meant the cheapest term premium this year or the lowest net cost policy after a number of years. It could also have meant a number of other things. He only said "cheapest"; he did not clarify it any further for me. I told him I would make a study and Illustration 7-2 is that exposition.

The letters at the top of the columns were put there to disguise the companies while in the actual proposal, I had the names of the companies. I have changed it here so as not to embarrass any company. Policies "B" and "C" were term and policy "C(2)" was graded premium life. All the others were a form of increasing premium whole life. I thought the best buy in the crowd was "C(2)" since it gave the best return for the dollars paid by the twentieth year. It also had the highest continuing coverage (paid up insurance). I did not illustrate the continuing coverage of the other policies because they were insignificant next to "C(2)."

My purpose was to sell something. I wanted to steer him to what I thought was the best policy but I wanted to make a display which showed as much detail as I felt was necessary for him to make a proper decision. "C(2)" had the earliest cash value and I showed that by putting the amounts next to the tenth and fifteenth years. Another reason I did that was to make the comparison to "A," "D," and "E" which did not have a cash value until the sixteenth year. These same three plans, 'A," "D," and "E" eventually had the highest premiums. You can study the illustration closely and find your own points of difference or similarity.

For his reasons Art chose "D." Clearly, comparing "D" to "C(2)," the latter looks better in premium by the sixteenth year, it develops more cash value earlier, and it generates as much cash value as premium by the twentieth year ($534,780-$549,680). Knowing the man's finances, I felt he made the wrong decision, but I sensed he was resolute in that decision. He made it strictly on a matter of early premium. I did not protest and wrote the app with that company.

The important thing was getting him as a client. It was not too much of a burden preparing this kind of display showing five companies with six policies on one sheet of paper. Also, the premium for the case was no small amount. I was compensated adequately and I still remain the agent who, with proper service, will get all future business whether it is with this insurance company or another.

Another benefit of this kind of proposal is the fact of having the choice among policies as opposed to either buying or not buying. The fatal alternative choice here was what company to choose and not a yes or no to owning any policy. It is a funny business we are in when we have to play mind games with our clients. We know they need the insurance—they know they need the insurance. Yet we have to use all kinds of psychological ploys to sell it on any basis, let alone the right basis.

Illustration 7-2

Art R. | **Face Amount $2,000,000**

Year	A	B	C	C(2)	D	E	
1	$4,950	$4,985	$7,750	$8,145		$3,540	$3,550
2	5,950	5,445	8,350	10,785		4,320	4,490
3	6,830	6,405	9,030	13,685		5,240	5,530
4	8,190	7,945	9,650	16,865		6,240	7,190
5	9,570	9,225	10,450	20,145		7,440	9,330
6	11,830	10,345	11,370	23,365		8,440	12,070
7	14,190	11,505	12,310	26,085		9,540	15,870
8	18,590	13,445	13,390	28,665		10,800	17,010
9	23,010	15,245	14,510	31,065		12,200	20,910
10	27,530	17,245	15,710	33,265	(equity 115,960)	13,720	25,830
11	34,410	19,185	17,010	35,205		16,440	31,810
12	41,770	21,705	18,390	37,065		19,520	39,390
13	49,130	24,305	19,910	38,785		23,000	48,470
14	56,510	27,065	21,490	40,205		27,000	60,130
15	63,850	30,125	23,270	41,705	(equity 296,620)	31,500	74,410

16	71,230	32,685	25,210	43,025		38,240	87,810
17	78,590	35,465	27,350	40,065		48,980	87,810
18	86,430	36,405	29,710	37,065		60,420	87,810
19	94,290	41,945	32,290	34,065		72,600	87,810
20	102,130	45,465	35,070	31,185		85,540	87,810
20-Year Premiums	$808,980	$416,140	$351,700	$549,680		$504,720	$815,040
20-Year Continuing Insurance		-0-	-0-	940,000			
20-Year Equity	162,000 no equity until year 16	-0- at 20 years at age 75– $4,000 cash value	-0-	534,780		154,000 no equity until year 16	426,000 no equity until year 16

There are very few individuals who object to our product on religious grounds, even though there are those who say, "I don't believe in it." All the other objections come down to a matter of premium, whether or no to pay any and, if so, how much and when. Therefore, when someone says they want the cheapest insurance, I show this type of illustration. Inherent in the warning of wanting the cheapest, we must read between the lines to see that the prospect has already looked at other plans with someone else. As a result, I want to show a low premium policy somewhere on the sheet just to let the prospect know I do represent him or her and not any one particular insurance company.

Every investment ever made is merely a function of time and money. This holds true for the bet at the race track, investing in the volatile world of commodity options, savings accounts, or life insurance. In life insurance the functions of time and money break down into two main laws with which we operate: the law of large numbers and; the law of compound interest. The large number aspect is known as mortality, and the compound interest segment comes into the areas of investment earnings and loading expenses of doing business.

There is nothing else. It is just a matter of when the money comes in, when it gets paid out, and what it does in the meantime. There is not too much difference between a term insurance premium schedule for a period of years and the same type of schedule for whole life. There is only a reversal of when the higher amounts will be paid. This falls into the realm of objections we get from our clients and prospects, but the "use of money" concept is important. The question is whether or not the insurance company can use it better for the problems of protection and savings then can the policyowner. All of us have access to company computers which verify the efficiency of the combination of dollars of protection and savings as with any whole life policy. With a term policy and side fund approach, the investment income has to be spectacular to equal what can be done by putting the side fund with the insurance company in one combined contract. In the last sentence I only considered the cost aspect; I will not get into the areas of self-discipline, taxation, and continuing coverage at advanced ages when term premiums either go out of sight or out of existence.

Labels and names are sometimes accurate and sometimes not. The advertising and sales approaches from some of us during the past five years or so has brought the title of "Term" insurance right to the top of the insurance module in client's minds. "Term" means cheap, but as I discussed earlier, does it mean cheap today or cost efficient for the duration of the policy? Unfortunately, for some, mind attention is short and now is now and then is then. Too many look only at the first year's premium and make a decision to make a decision later. This means "get the coverage now and make a decision regarding the best policy later." Therefore, even though I have spoken about not using the names of policies, the time does present itself when the discussion hones in on the hard theme of "Term."

Then, when there is no choice but to discuss "Term" straight up, I use Illustration 7-3. I prepare the proposal with the direct title, "Term Insurance" as you can see on the sheet. The amount of insurance is $1,000,000 and I have detailed this case for a period of twenty-five years. There is nothing unusual about the first twenty-five lines; they merely show the term insurance premium for this man, John Jones. I go on to show the total premium, total equity, which is zero, and the continuing coverage which is also zero. But then I throw in two enticing riders. The first is waiver of premium which is always welcome by the prospects. I purposely do not show it in the insurance premiums so I can make a special point of showing and discussing it, in detail, at the bottom of the illustration. Here it is demonstrated as $450 per year on an accelerating basis.

The second rider is one I call "Equity Builder." If you are searching your mind or your computer discs for such a rider, don't go any further. It is a name I made-up. It does look enticing to see something that has no cost; in fact, it requires $306,785 less premium and creates an equity of $467,950. I merely read the details as you see them under point "2)." It never fails to bring forward questions about how this rider works, which requires less premium and creates cash value where none existed before. My answer to the client, and to you, is to look at Illustration 7-4.

The column labelled "Term Insurance" is a repeat of what appears in Illustration 7-3. The next column called "Equity Builder" is the net premium of whatever Whole Life plan you wish to show. In this example, I was showing Graded Premium 20. Under the columns I totaled the premiums. The first is the same as it was on the previous illustration; the second is the cumulative premiums for the cash value policy. Here you will see the amounts of $791,570 versus $484,785 which comes to a difference of $306,785 and which I showed under the "Equity Builder" option at the bottom of the "Term Insurance" illustration.

Illustration 7-3

John Jones	Face Amount $1,000,000
Year	**Term Insurance**
1	$7,280
2	7,930
3	8,710
4	9,420
5	10,340
6	11,360
7	12,430
8	13,540
9	14,740
10	15,960
11	17,390
12	19,190
13	21,630
14	24,150
15	26,580
16	29,060
17	31,560
18	34,410
19	37,240
20	40,410
21	44,080
22	48,560
23	54,130
24	59,900
25	66,220
Total Premium	$791,570
Total Equity	-0-
Total Continuing Coverage—No Premium	-0-

Riders Available:
1) Waiver of Premium—$450 yr. (accelerating)
2) Equity Builder—no cost—($306,785 less premium) (equity created—$467, 950)

March 1984

Illustration 7-4

	John Jones	Face Amount $1,000,000
Year	**Term Insurance**	**Equity Builder**
1	$7,280	$13,885
2	7,930	14,870
3	8,710	15,395
4	9,420	15,935
5	10,340	16,505
6	11,360	17,065
7	12,430	17,615
8	13,540	18,145
9	14,740	18,655
10	15,960	19,155
11	17,390	19,655
12	19,190	20,115
13	21,630	20,535
14	24,150	20,935
15	26,580	21,375
16	29,060	21,785
17	31,560	22,185
18	34,410	22,545
19	37,240	22,915
20	40,410	23,085
21	44,080	23,215
22	48,560	21,935
23	54,130	20,315
24	59,900	19,035
25	66,220	17,925
Total Premium	$791,570	$484,785
Total Equity	-0-	467,950
Continuing Coverage—No Premium	-0-	608,000

March 1984

I then display the total equity for both options. Of course, the "Term Insurance" has none and the Graded Premium has $467,950, in this case. This verifies what I showed before regarding lower premiums and equity creation. The "Continuing Coverage-No Premium" demonstrates the presence, or lack of, paid up insurance. This is another plus for the "Equity Builder" plan no matter what type of cash value contract it is.

This has been a forcefully effective proposal for me. What I have done is show the prospect what has been asked of me, Term Insurance. Then I throw in the zinger which is the essence of Whole Life—lower overall premiums and higher overall cash. Yet I have done this without mentioning any kind of permanent plan. I leave it to the curiosity or enlightened self-interest of the buyer to ask what kind of rider will provide such magic. You and I know there is no such rider and all I am discussing is the difference between the natures of these two types of plans, but the prospect's mind has become opened on his or her terms and at his or her volition. Then it is a matter of research and not a matter of being sold something through the initiative of a salesperson. It is purely voluntary to go forward with the examination of the second illustration.

As I mentioned, there is no difference between term premiums and whole life premiums; there is only a reversal of the schedules. It is a function of time and money or "use of money" as some would say. Technically, there is a whopping difference and it is on the side of the permanent product rather than the temporary one. However, I leave it to the prospect to discover that by his or her own reasoning, after they have asked me to explain such a miraculous rider. To be even more technical, the permanent plan costs less overall and, even at its peak, does not come close to what the temporary plan will require in the later years when paying those types of charges becomes murderous.

This chapter was entitled *Price May Vary* and we have seen it sure can. Our job is to give the clientele exactly what they want. In the course of doing that the price will vary. If someone legitimately wants the lower price spread, it is our duty to provide just that. Our obligation, though, is to bring forward all the factors of now and tomorrow which, taken together, cause the price to vary. The result will be the placement of precisely the kind of insurance that is right for the current situations. The price may vary; the questions are: when; for whose benefit; and with what result?

8

See Me Later

There are certain things that can be done on the first try and there are certain things that require repeated efforts. This pertains in business as it does to all things in life. In our business there are agents who work on a one interview system and there are those who have a pattern of two, or three, or more interviews to complete their process.

In certain aspects of daily involvement, there is no way to accomplish a task on one try even though, conceptually, it is possible. As an example, think of all the times you were doing a household chore which required something from the hardware store. This is a task which should be accomplished without error, but it just isn't in the cards. Let us assume you are putting metal shelving into your garage. You have geared up mentally to the task and you are all ready to finish the job so you can get on with the rest of your Sunday. You make the trip to the hardware store prepared to buy the shelves, brackets, nuts, bolts, and other equipment needed for this task.

Upon arriving at the correct aisle, you find your life has been made even easier than you had expected. You think, "These people are really great. They anticipate what an amateur needs and produce it completely." Why all this exuberance? Standing right in front of you is an assembled shelving unit; exactly what you need. You can picture yourself constructing this thing and mounting it to the back wall so it doesn't topple. In your mind's eye the job is done and it's good. The price is reasonable and you walk out with a bulky, but welcome, box anxiously yearning to get home and feel the satisfaction when the job is finished and your spouse pats you on the back. You wrestle the monster into your car and are off to your home.

You study the instructions in the box which show the schematics of getting this miniature Golden Gate Bridge together and decide it isn't that tough, so you get started. The work is fairly easy and you are breezing along putting the struts, shelves, nuts and bolts together when, suddenly, you realize there aren't enough nuts and bolts. You tear the carton apart and there is not another cellophane package to be found. You separate the metal shelving but there just is nothing else. A little under-the-breath muttering and you are off to the hardware store again with a set of nuts and bolts so you don't make a mistake and buy the wrong size. The store is out of the ones you need so you compromise and buy the closest size you can find. Eventually, the job gets done but it exemplifies one of the unwritten laws of household puttering: you can't finish a small job in one try.

I see this all the time with my all girl family of my wife, Sharon, and four daughters. It seems there is more activity of going back to the stores because of wrong sizes, wrong colors, and other reasons than there was for things bought in the first place. Just last year, as every year, Sharon informed me shortly after Thanksgiving that all of her Christmas and Hanukkah shopping was finished. As usual, that was another of Aesop's Fables because, when the night before Christmas comes, there will still be one more item that the store is out of which they promised would be in stock in plenty of time.

The government is a prime example of both time and cost overrun inefficiency. Money and time excesses are standard operating procedure. The government is one segment where it is impossible to complete any job in just one trip. This is true no matter how large the office or how many bodies there are to, supposedly, run it efficiently. I will give you this example. A short while ago, I lost my wallet which, among other things, contained my driver's license and my American Express card. For the credit card, the routine turned out to be just routine. My secretary called the number which was printed at the bottom of the statement and was informed that all charge privileges would be stopped immediately by computer and a new card would be in the mail within a week. One phone call and no further need for showing up at a formal session anywhere. Incidentally, the card came on time as promised.

For the secretary of state's office, I sat down and thought what could go wrong. I anticipated a long list of possible foul-ups and red tape. I knew where the local office was and I fully expected to show up and apply for a duplicate license. That made all the sense in the world to me. But I had this feeling in my computer(stomach) that I'd best prepare myself for a frustrating experience. It seemed natural the first step should be the same as dealing with a profit making concern, such as the credit card company. I had my secretary call to determine the drill. She called from 9:30 a.m. to 2:30 p.m. and received a busy signal all that time. We also checked the possibility of a phone malfunction but the phone company told us all was in order; it was simply a matter of a busy phone.

At 3:00 p.m. I felt I should go over to the state office, otherwise I would be driving over the weekend without any proof of eligibility. I waited my turn in line and finally got up to the counter. The clerk politely, but matter-of-factly, asked me for three items of identification. I told her that most were stolen along with the wallet, but she informed me she could get in trouble unless she saw the three items. I told her I was now frustrated because I attempted to avoid this type of hassle by calling in advance but the line was busy all the time. She agreed they had an inadequate phone system but, all the same, I had to reappear with the needed identification. She gave me the proper form and told me to come back.

The next day I arrived at nine o'clock and was the fourth person in line outside on the sidewalk before the doors had even opened. I had three pieces of identification with me. When the doors opened, the three other people went to the "New Licenses" section so I was first in the "Forms" section. The young lady waited on me and everything went smoothly. While I was in front of her, the phone rang. She picked it up and did not lose a beat while continuing to work on my forms. She didn't use any form of polite greeting but rattled into the mouthpiece, "Southfield, please hold." She put the phone on hold and, without any evidence of getting back to it, went on with what she was doing. I know I always get a little nervous when I have someone on hold or have two people expecting service from me, both at the same time. I looked at my watch and saw 9:02 a.m. Another day was off and stalling.

These little stories tell of the bungling and delaying in government and business but it is not only a story of someone else's inefficiencies. We've got problems in our business, too. Unfortunately, the agencies and the home offices give the same types of services. It has become worse in recent years and I think the chief culprit is the lack of training. I hear the same sort of complaint from clients as I have just related to you. In addition to the lack of proper training, there is the twin villain of lack of accountability. Be all of that as it may, my purpose here is to outline the waste which comes as a result from not being prepared or, even if one is adequately prepared, having to redo a process. I believe the inadequacies are not as great in the commission selling field because time is money and good service saves time and makes money.

My main thrust is to delineate the necessity for the return call. For us as insurance salespeople that translates into, "See me later" or " I want to think it over." Hopefully, the dietetic illustrations shown in this book will eliminate some of the delays by focusing on what is important. Yet the fact of life is delays and call backs are a part of our business. Not every interview ends in a sale and not every interview closes the first time you ask for the order. If they did, we probably would lose some of our conscientiousness and end up in the same bag as those I just accused for lack of attentiveness.

Ours is still a business of great numbers. We must have a tremendous volume of names in order to reclassify them as prospects and, eventually, cull them as clients. I believe everyone has heard of the *One Card System.* This is a method of obtaining and classifying prospects and clients so the onus is taken off making sales and is put on the attention to the details of processing large numbers of names. The names are placed on cards and certain service and selling functions are performed regularly and periodically. Points are given by performing these functions regardless of what the results are in respect to sales. The philosophy is that the sales will come as a by-product of the real product of names. As a result, the processing of names in this orderly fashion is the job at hand and not that of making sales.

This system only exemplifies what we should all know about our business. It is strictly a process of seeing enough people. No matter what method you use, you have to make enough attempts in order to have a closing ratio which is successful for you. No calls-no sales. Some calls-some sales. Lots of calls-lots of sales. But among these measurements, no matter what your method is, comes the time of the call back. Some of the requests to see someone at a later time are merely excuses to get rid of the salesperson at that particular moment. The purpose is for the prospect to regroup his or her thinking so the momentum can be recouped from the salesperson. Some are a pure sham which comes with the inability to say either "yes" or "no." Some are purely procrastination.

No matter what they are, we must accept them as part of our business and not lose our temper with the prospect. After all, in the final analysis, it was we and not they who made the initial call. It was we who asked for the appointment. Therefore, we have no right to express anger or disgust to them. They have the right to do exactly as they please. We can disagree or disapprove but we have to either keep it to ourselves, or express it as tactfully as possible within the framework of counselor selling and not that of pushing a product.

Everyone has some system for processing the names from which we call. Whether one has prospecting methods which requires hundreds of names, or works in the ultra-sophisticated markets where only a few candidates are needed, there still has to be some way of keeping track of the name gathering, calls, and results. Some people use elaborate records while others use the *One Card System*. Some record all events in ledgers and others use a system of elimination whereby the records are thrown away as soon as there is a negative response; this includes any paperwork and the name itself.

I am one of those who likes to get rid of the thoughts of anything I have decided is of no value. I do not process large numbers of names. I work in the advanced market of estate, business, and retirement planning and I do my prospecting on a referral and personal observation basis. However, in working in this so-called advanced market, there comes the attendant items of follow-up which requires large segments of time and attention to detail. As a result, there must be fastidious attention to all the parts of running a tax/insurance type of business. Toward this end, there must be ways of keeping things in their proper sequence and doing all the parts in a timely order.

The first rule I have regarding my desk work is there is never more than one file or case on my desk at any one time. I find if I allow too many things to get in my line of vision, I scatter my concentration by spotting something other than the matter at hand. Consequently, I will pick up the stray file or letter and start thinking about something new. Under my method, my concentration is focused and I can complete one job before I even think about another. Incidentally, I do a great deal of work at my desk as you have seen from the shrunken illustrations. They require I put a lot of time into the planning so that the interviews are short and, hopefully, sweet.

I also have the rule that no one can put anything on my desk. I also never put anything on anyone else's desk. You might wonder how any business ever gets transacted in a system where nothing can pass from place to place. Obviously, everyone is not at their desks all the time so how does correspondence, mail, memos, and instructions get transmitted from person to person? The answer is all deliveries are placed on the seats. I put anything I am giving to anyone else on their chair and their instructions to me are the same.

By putting things on the seats instead of the desks it keeps the piles down and also reduces the chances of items from one file getting into another. We have all had the sad experience of looking in every corner of our office trying to find a certain letter or piece of paper. The usual questions are, "Where could it be?" and "Who had it last?" Finally, we give up and do without, or reduplicate the errant item only to have it turn up someday when we least expect it and in a file where we have no idea of how it got there.

Another question which may come to mind is where do all these files and correspondence go if there is never more than one case on the desk at any one time? I have arranged one of the drawers in the credenza behind me in a file system labeled "Monday, Tuesday, Wednesday, Thursday, Friday," and "Saturday." When I get back to my desk after being away, or when something comes in for me, I place it in the appropriate day's file. On that day when the item comes forward I take the action which is necessary to complete the job or prepare it for the next step and I will never have to do that step again. This also leads to the result of only touching one piece of paper one time.

Each morning, I open the drawer for that day, list the files which are there onto Illustration 8-1 and then put the file back in the day's slot. Some people have said to me I am wasting time by picking up the file and making a list; they say I could have saved time by actually doing the work and moving the file on to the next person. In reality and experience, this has not proven to be correct. I find each minute I spend preparing Illustration 8-1 saves me ten to fifteen more. The reason for this is I try not to think as I am doing my listing; my job at that moment is to organize the day so I can work it in an efficient manner. Later, I will bring up that file and put it on the desk for whatever the job.

Illustration 8-1 is a form which I have developed. There is nothing sacred or magical about it other than the fact it works for me. There are a myriad of other daytimers or other organizers which work equally well or even better. The point is everyone should have a plan of what the day is going to look like. No one would start a cross-country trip without a map.

Illustration 8-1

BRODE, LANDSBERG, MEISEL & HAAS

	APPOINTMENTS	DATE PHONE CALLS	THINGS THAT MUST BE DONE
7:30			
8:00			
8:30			
9:00			
9:30			
10:00			
10:30			
11:00			
11:30			
12:00			
12:30			
1:00			
1:30			THINGS THAT SHOULD BE DONE
2:00			
2:30			
3:00			
3:30			
4:00			
4:30			
EVENING			

The paper is nothing more than a second sheet on our company letterhead. I have taken a sample to the printer and had them printed in packs of 250, which are glued on the end in the form of a pad of paper. I have also had two holes punched in the pad so I can mount the whole thing in a holder which was a gift to me from one of my daughters. She conveniently purchased the holder at an office supply store. This is what sits on my desk; a pad of daily organizers.

The first column is called, "Appointments" and shows the day broken into half-hour increments. It also lists "Evening" at the bottom for any appointments or social engagements I might have. As you can see, I start the day at 7:30 a.m.

The center column has an area where I letter in the "Date;" below that is "Phone Calls." Here I put all the calls I know I have to make. There is a box on the left side of the column which I formerly used to check off the calls when they were completed. I no longer use that column but I will explain what I do use in Illustration 8-3. (I have never had the form reprinted as it still serves my purpose very adequately.) You will notice the column is only half a page long. Although I usually have more phone calls, which spill over the boxes, I have decided against more lines because I want room to make notes or take instructions. You can quickly see this one sheet is the only form of organization I use. I hate carrying bulky things and I don't even carry a regular wallet. My wallet consists of one of those small card size calculator/alarm clocks and the case to hold it. In the case I carry a small amount of cash, one credit card, my driver's license, my health club card and small notes as necessary. I don't have my old draft card, voting card, combination to my old high school locker, pictures, or other paper which I never use.

The top half of the third column is "Things That Must Be Done;" the lower half is "Things That Should Be Done." It is obvious to you why these are used. I list the vital things that must be done on that day and I do them. The "Should Be Done's get taken care of as time allows. Mind you, anything at the bottom half will eventually turn up at the top half, but they are not vital and will not take away from the important items.

Illustration 8-2 is the way a typical day looks when the items are filled in. You will see the appointments for the day, including racquetball at 5:30 p.m. I have disguised the names and phone numbers but you can see how I list them. By the way, this was a typical day and I did use this sheet.

I just put in a code which meant something to me, but also allowed me to tear it off at the end of the day so I could write about it at night.

The vital thing which had to be done was Don F.'s summary which was due a week later. Remember from a previous chapter that I usually work about a week in advance. This allows for the travel schedule I keep. It also allows sufficient time for the secretaries to prepare things for me and get it back in time for me to "feel the laces."

Under the "Should Be Done's" you will notice two items which were not vital but were on my mind to be taken care of. The license was to replace the one I lost that I discussed before. The print shop was to look at some proofs for a new project I am publishing. Now look at Illustration 8-3 to see what was actually accomplished for the day.

This is what I call the "Blue Line Special." In editing terms to blue line something is to strike it out and that is precisely what I try to do every day. I lay out plans for myself and my main goal is to live up to what I expected of myself when my mind was clear and I was in the "Employer" mode. I use a blue highlighter and strike through each item as I complete it. My objective is to finish off this piece of paper this day so I can throw it away. I have no desire to save these things because, if I have done my work right, each item is either in a different mode and will show up later for another process, or is completed and is filed away permanently. It is rare that I fully blue line one of these daily organizers so I have to move some names to the following day. This is pure waste because I wish I had finished everything the day before. Sometimes it can't be helped but, for sure, the reason is not that I didn't try. I hate having to write the same thing twice and that serves as a deterrent to me for goofing-off.

You can tell I finished all of the phone calls with the exception of "Ystace" and "Robert Zswart." There were two added as the day progressed, "Saford" and "Kosar." When calls come in that I can't take right away, I list them here so I do not forget to make them. When the secretary hands me one of those phone message sheets, I try to make the call right away, but if I can't complete it, I list it on this one control sheet. Next to "Sinai, Manko" and "Steve" you will see arrows leading away from their names. This means I will call them back. Next to "Rishv" you will see the arrow points to his name. This means the first phone call I made to him was left with the message to return my call. The arrow means he has to take the action. Actually, this was a pretty good day since

Illustration 8-2

BRODE, LANDSBERG, MEISEL & HAAS

	APPOINTMENTS
7:30	MANDER
8:00	
8:30	
9:00	STEVE R
9:30	
10:00	
10:30	
11:00	
11:30	
12:00	
12:30	
1:00	
1:30	
2:00	
2:30	
3:00	
3:30	
4:00	
4:30	

EVENING

5:30 RAQUETBALL

DATE 12/10/84 PHONE CALLS
353-9500 SINAI
528-0983 CHRIS
JUAN LIPE
155-7100 RISHV
077-7908 URZW
YSTACE
RICH
JERRY KAUFMAN
ROBERT ZSWART 077-8097
358-1276 KEN MANKO
GANTSON
STEVE RE

1. HARTFORD
2. YEE
3. LOTTS
4. MARK

THINGS THAT MUST BE DONE
DON F. SUMMAR

THINGS THAT SHOULD BE DONE
NEW DRIVERS LICENSE
PRINT SHOP

Illustration 8-3

BRODE, LANDSBERG, MEISEL & HAAS

DATE 12/10/84

	APPOINTMENTS	PHONE CALLS	THINGS THAT MUST BE DONE
7:30	MANDER	353-9500 SINAI	DON F. SUMMARY
8:00		528-0983 CHRIS	CHUCK LOTTS ASSOM MFM FORM
8:30		JUAN LIPE	
9:00	STEVE R	155-7100 RISHV	
9:30		077-7908 URZW	
10:00		YSTACE	
10:30		RICH	
11:00		JERRY KAUFMAN	
11:30		ROBERT ZSWART 077-8097	
12:00		358-1276 KEN MANKO	
12:30		GANTSON	
1:00		STEVE RE	
1:30			
2:00			
2:30			
3:00			
3:30			
4:00			
4:30			

1. HARTFORD
2. YEE
3. LOTTS
4. MARK

GEORGE SAFORD
218-7652

BRUCE KOSAR
358-1281

THINGS THAT SHOULD BE DONE
NEW DRIVERS LICENSE
PRINT SHOP

EVENING

5:30 RAQUETBALL

I completed most of the calls I set out to make. Of course, there were many other calls which came in that I took.

In the last sections, I managed to have time to complete everything that must or should have been done. I consider this to be a good day. When I leave for home and there are still things or calls to be completed, it is a very simple thing to fold this sheet into thirds, put it into my suit coat, and do the work at home if I want or care to.

Remember the title of this chapter. My goal with this sheet is to process names and tasks as they come due. When I do all the things I have set out for myself, it is simply a matter of honesty and dedication to fulfillment. If I stall or procrastinate, I will eventually pay the price. This one control sheet is my way of keeping busy. I don't care if everything I did that day was wrong or if every call was a loser. The important thing is I did it all. I give myself all the credit for having completed the sheet. The results make no difference to the immediate aim of setting out all those things which had to be done and then doing them. It makes it more pleasant if all the jobs were winning efforts, but tomorrow is another day and I can set up another list of things to be done.

I don't even care if one day's list is a short one. If I complete it, I was successful and I have no feelings of guilt because I succeeded in what I put up as my tasks for that day. I was true to myself as the employee in that I accomplished the whole work schedule. I wrote it down and I attempted, in all good faith, to do it all.

There are three times I can think of when one should be honest with himself or herself. These are, first, when you are jogging or walking. Your mind becomes clear with the relaxation and the euphoria. Secondly, when you are driving on a long trip your mind gets on autopilot and the thoughts are clear; ones which are usually sound. The third is when you awaken in the middle of the night, for no good reason, and have a brainstorm. In all of these events, you should record or write down what the thought was and then transfer it to your job sheet. Then if someone says, "See me later," you will be content in the knowledge you did everything you could do when you should have done it. The "later" becomes a fresh attempt because you did all you could do and at the right time.

9

Put It In Writing

Have you ever gone out on an interview to pick up a small balance of a premium because of a miscalculation, or to get a form signed, or to perform some other service function, and get involved in a conversation, or in some other way get sidetracked and forget to get completed the very item for which you went? I have, and it is one of the world's biggest wastes of time. I have been mighty angry with myself when I had to repeat the visit or send something in the mail which I could have done in person on the first attempt. It is natural to get so intensely involved in the dramatics of an interview some of the parts are forgotten. Especially so if it is a case encompassing many parts of estate, business, or retirement planning.

When we were kids and were going to the store our mothers would pin a note to our shirts or jackets so there was no thinking related to the chore. She did the brainwork and we did the legwork. Well, unless Mama is in business with you and takes care of every interview, you're on your own. You have to do all the parts so it makes sense to minimize the legwork and maximize the brainy stuff.

After many experiences of goofing-up on small details, which the home office would not forgive, I decided I would try to be more efficient and adopt the parent-child method of writing myself notes. I wrote these notes in my office and then carefully read them when I arrived at the job site. There really is nothing new under the sun. Somehow, every brand-new discovery has a beginning some other place at some other time. Mama's method still works. In the old days, the grocer also liked it because he didn't have to rely on junior's memory and then hope a job, which could have been done in one visit, didn't result in someone else coming back to the store for an exchange or some other reparation. I think if I didn't come in with the note he would wait on me warily and anticipate someone coming back later to correct for the error of sending a kid to the store without a note. I wonder what the clients think of us when we have to come back and finish a poorly done detail.

I have adopted this idea of improving the odds for success by writing down the chores to be done. My friend, George Steinberger, CLU, used to relate to me that, when he worked for one of the auto companies in Detroit, there was a code which the employees used as a watchword among them: "AVO," which meant "Avoid Verbal Orders." The average elephant eats about three hundred pounds of food each day and only retains about five percent. I don't know if this has any parallel with the old adage that an elephant never forgets, but I always wondered how much an elephant ever had to remember. No matter, whether it is food or data, we just don't retain much. There is so much to remember when we are dealing with clients in the advanced markets that it doesn't make any sense not to give advance thought and preparation to a case. For myself, I write down everything; I wouldn't cross the street to see a client without marking down the things I had to do. I don't trust anyone else's memory and I especially don't trust mine.

A sponsor would never allow a commercial to be done if it were not scripted out in advance. What are the sponsors attempting to accomplish? I assure you they are not bringing us the shows for any civic or philanthropic motives. They are trying to sell products and make a profit. I sure would not call the home office with any special instructions for a case and expect to get the case issued in the fashion I relayed to the listener. There are too many chances for error; either voice errors or listening errors or many other combinations. If I want something issued in a specific, but unusual, fashion I write the instructions on the application in the memo section or, just like Mama used to do, I send along a note.

I do the same thing for myself and my clients on every single meeting. I prepare an agenda of what has to be done at that meeting. I sit in my office during the brainstorming period and prepare a list of all the things that have to be done and all the things I would like to have happen. This is an abbreviated listing of the details of the interview and it is not meant to be a script. I do not try to be detailed about what I am going to say at this point of the agenda construction. I throw in everything which pertains to the case. After I have written down everything, I will go back and elaborate, cut, change, reorganize, tighten up and, generally, prepare a presentable outline of what this meeting is designed to accomplish, both for the client or prospect and for the agent. At this point, neatness doesn't count and I make no effort to have things in, what will be, the final order. I only want to get everything in so, even at this stage of preparation, I do not forget my purpose.

In addition to all the items I want in the agenda, I leave one or two blank numbers. This indicates I do not intend to avoid any new items which will be brought up; in fact, I welcome them. When questions come, I have the option of answering them right then or saying, "That's a good question and I know the answer. Please put it under number six so we don't forget it." Or I can say, "I don't know the answer. Let's both write it down on the agenda so I don't forget to research it and get back to you with the explanation." Something else then starts happening; the client becomes a part of the meeting. There is no way to sit back and not participate when there is a schedule to follow and it takes some thinking on the part of all parties. I also plant places where I want questions to come so I can force the other parties to become a part of the interview.

I do this agenda for selling, delivery, or service interviews. I prepare one for all the people who will be attending the meeting. In this way I convey the idea that this is a business meeting and not just a monologue on my part. I explain to them this agenda will serve a few needs. It will keep me on track, it will take the shortest possible time, since we are organized in advance, it will allow for questions and answers, and it will be a permanent record of what is being discussed. The CPA or attorney can then look back to see what was being advised in the areas in which we were working. I instruct them to three-hole punch the agenda when we are finished and put it into the corporate minute book, including their notes in their own handwriting. Who ever said corporate minutes had to be prose?

Let us now get to some examples of the agendas I have used for actual cases. The names will be disguised but, I assure you, these are actual interviews. Illustration 9-1 is a sample of the yellow pad copy of my notes as I was getting ready for a meeting with Don and Dorothy Ra and their advisors. The purpose for the meeting was a general review of the estate and business situation with special emphasis being placed on the possibility of the establishment of an irrevocable trust for the ownership of existing insurance. The CPA's were the ones who had stimulated the meeting and there was a letter which had gone to the clients, Stu Sinai, the attorney, and me. I personally felt the existing insurance should not be put in the trust since it had other work to do and that would be the thrust

Illustration 9-1

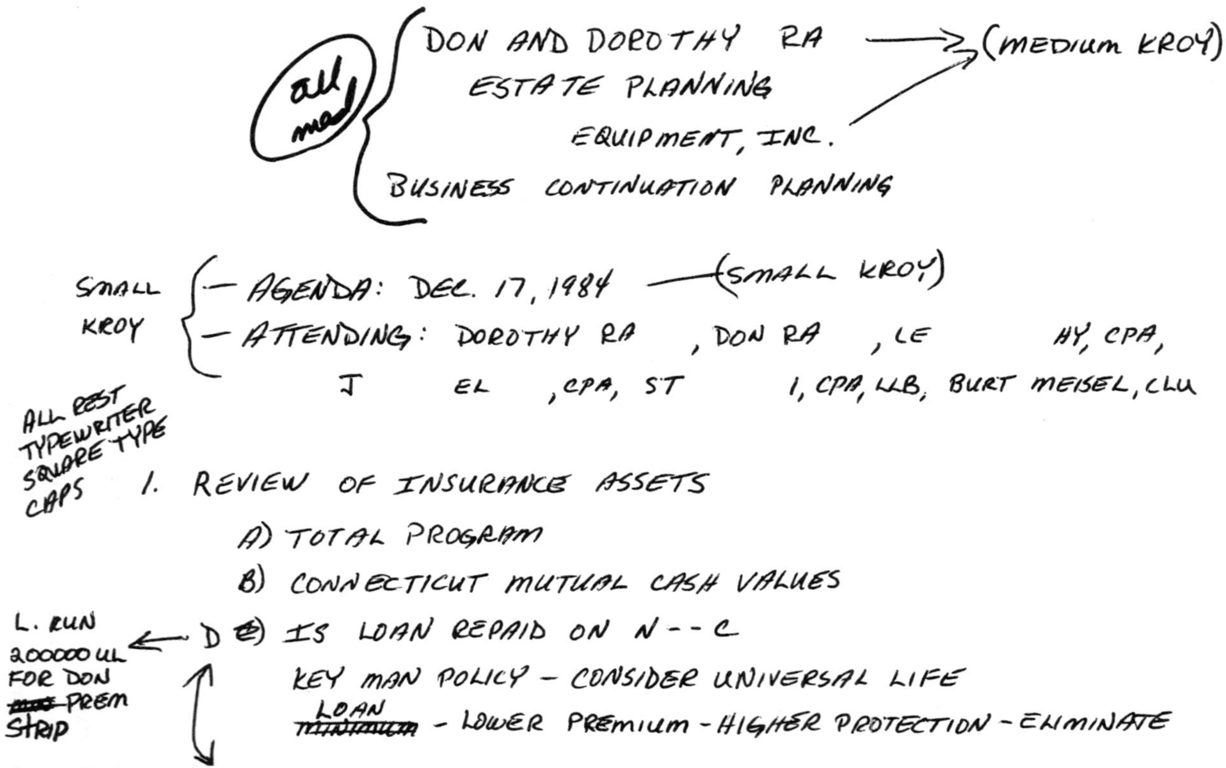

(all med)
DON AND DOROTHY RA → (MEDIUM KROY)
ESTATE PLANNING
EQUIPMENT, INC.
BUSINESS CONTINUATION PLANNING

SMALL KROY
— AGENDA: DEC. 17, 1984 — (SMALL KROY)
— ATTENDING: DOROTHY RA , DON RA , LE HY, CPA,
J EL , CPA, ST I, CPA, LLB, BURT MEISEL, CLU

ALL REST TYPEWRITER SQUARE TYPE CAPS
1. REVIEW OF INSURANCE ASSETS
A) TOTAL PROGRAM
B) CONNECTICUT MUTUAL CASH VALUES
L. RUN 200000 UL FOR DON ~~PREM~~ PREM STRIP ← D ~~C~~) IS LOAN REPAID ON N - - C
KEY MAN POLICY — CONSIDER UNIVERSAL LIFE
~~MINIMUM~~ LOAN — LOWER PREMIUM — HIGHER PROTECTION — ELIMINATE

L, DO YOU HAVE LEDGERS COMPARING TWO WAYS. SHOW TO ME.
WE'LL DO CUT AND PASTE OF "TOTAL CASH VALUE" COLUMN
cut CV colum VLR or not or show

C) INCREASE IN DON AND DOROTHY POLICIES UNDER VLIR

2. LIQUIDITY NEEDS FOR DON AND DOROTHY

A) ~~[illegible]~~ TAX PROBLEM AT SECOND DEATH

ESTATE -	2,300,000
LESS EXEMPTION -	600,000
LESS ADMINISTRATION - $ DEBTS, ETC.	100,000
TAXABLE ESTATE	1,600,000
TAXES	550,000

(8-4-82)

B) DISPLAY OF GROWTH SINCE 1982 - SEE GRAPHIC

C) LONGEVITY TABLES - MALE 65 - 14.0 YRS, FEMALE 65 18.4 YRS

D) CONSIDER DISCOUNTING TAXES - UNDER SECOND DEATH PLANNING (REFER LESHIES LETTER - 12/5/84 ¶4. L.4)

a) 500,000 JOINT AND SUVIVOR PLAN PHOENIX MUTUAL PAYS AT SECOND DEATH (SEE ILLUSTRATIONS A + B)

b) CONNECTICUT MUTUAL - SEPARATE $150,000 POLICIES - OBJECT: CREATE IMMEDIATE FUND AT FIRST DEATH - GROWS AT INTEREST - KEEP PREMIUMS DOWN

L. RUN STRIP 150,000 AL L'S FOR BOTH

3.

4.

1 + 5 + 1

of my agenda. I called both the attorney and CPA's in advance to discuss this so we would not be at odds during the meeting and would have no clashes.

The client's were owners of a large sales and service organization. They were both in their mid-sixties and had two children, who had been gifted minor stock interests, working in the business. We had had many meetings through the years and the clients had always followed good advice. Already in place were agreements for Section 303 redemption, wills and trusts, deferred compensation, and a cross-purchase agreement between their children for the stock the children held. They were just coming off a very profitable business year after having had two very poor ones.

The top few lines of Illustration 9-1 outline the names of persons who will be at the meeting, the name of the company, and the date. At the upper right, there is a note which says, "MEDIUM KROY." This is a note to my secretary, Lori, who will be preparing the final copies, to use the Kroy machine which makes letters in different sizes or different type styles. She knows I want block letters to make the names of the individuals larger and more prominent. Everyone likes to see his or her name in print. To the left of the bracket you will see "all med." This is Lori's handwriting and is part of her notes for the preparation.

To the left and below the bracket you will see the note, "SMALL KROY." This is a further instruction on how I would like these lines to look. The left-hand instructions below that lets Lori know I want the rest of the agenda to be typewritten.

Item *1.* concerns a general review of all the insurance assets the corporation presently owns. *1A)* refers to a graphic I had prepared showing the total program. *1B)* showed the cash values on the Connecticut Mutual policies which I had sold for the purpose of business continuation planning. I made specific reference to these policies because I wanted to show the aspect of capital transfer due to the fact the policies were growing in cash value as quickly as the premiums were being paid. This would be an important item to discuss later when the question of whether or not to assign these policies to an irrevocable trust would be brought up by the CPA's. My point would be somebody has to pay something someday. Transferring the policies to the trust would not obviate premiums, but only put the onus on the insureds themselves rather than the corporation.

The next two items are labeled *1D)* and *1C.)* You will notice they have been struck over and were originally reversed. This is part of the editing which goes on once an agenda has been constructed. The reason for the change is because I felt it was more important to first show the improvement under the variable loan interest program for the existing policies before I got to a discussion of one key man policy (here noted as *"N——C")*. You can also observe the notes to Lori off to the left of the items. Next to *D*, I wrote "run $200,000 UL for Don min prem." The word "strip" replaces "min." This is Lori's note and represents the actual computer phrase for this type of illustration that shows no accumulation of cash value but just enough premium to keep the policy going.

Next to *C* I asked the question, "L. do you have ledgers comparing two ways. Show to me. We'll do cut and paste of 'total cash value' column." Below my handwriting you will see Lori has made a note of her own regarding how to handle the cut and paste method of comparing the original policy, which had an eight percent loan interest rate, and the new variable loan interest rate. Our thinking here was to do it on one sheet of paper by just running the two total cash value columns next to each other. This would lay further groundwork for the value of the life insurance to the overall planning since the companies had made improvements in policies since the time of issue. After all, we were dealing with two individuals in their sixties and it was valuable to show a lessening of premiums by the companies.

Point *2A)* showed calculations of the value of the estate and the taxes which would be due. I took the total value from the letter which we received from the accountants. They had not calculated the taxes so I did it. The purpose here was to show what the size of the estate was as officially figured by the accountants and then compare it, under item *B*, with what the estate was in 1982. Next to my lettering of item *2B,* Lori has lettered "(8-4-82)." She had searched the file and found the CPA's calculations from two years ago. As you can tell there were other reference pages which accompanied this appointment. However, we did not illustrate all the other items we had as part of the presentation.

Point *C* showed the mortality expectancies for the two clients. My purpose was to build for point *D* under which I would lead into a discussion of the need for liquidity on the second death. I did make reference to Leslie's (CPA) letter which discussed the same item.

Illustration 9-2

DON AND DOROTHY RA

ESTATE PLANNING

EQUIPMENT INC.

BUSINESS CONTINUATION PLANNING
AGENDA: DEC. 17, 1984

ATTENDING:

DOROTHY RA , DON RA , LE HY, CPA, J EL , CPA

ST I, CPA, LLB, BURT MIEISEL, CLU

1. REVIEW OF INSURANCE ASSETS
   - A. TOTAL PROGRAM
   - B. CONNECTICUT MUTUAL CASH VALUES
   - C. INCREASE IN DON AND DOROTHY POLICIES UNDER VLIR
   - D. IS LOAN REPAID ON N — C KEY MAN POLICY — CONSIDER UNIVERSAL LIFE — LOWER PREMIUM — HIGHER PROTECTION — ELIMINATE LOAN

2. LIQUIDITY NEEDS FOR DON AND DOROTHY

A. TAX PROBLEM AT SECOND DEATH

ESTATE	$2,300,000
LESS EXEMPTION	600,000
LESS ADMINISTRATION & DEPTS, ETC.	100,000
TAXABLE ESTATE	1,600,000
TAXES	550,000

B. DISPLAY OF GROWTH SINCE 1982 — SEE GRAPHIC

C. LONGEVITY TABLES — MALE 65 — 14 YRS, FEMALE 65 — 18.4 YRS

D. CONSIDER DISCOUNTING TAXES — UNDER SECOND DEATH PLANNING (REFER LESLIE'S LETTER — 12/5/84 PARAGRAPH 4, LINE 4)

a. $500,000 JOINT AND SURVIVOR PLAN PHOENIX MUTUAL PAYS AT SECOND DEATH (SEE ILLUSTRATION A AND B)

b. CONNECTICUT MUTUAL — SEPARATE $150,000 POLICIES — OBJECT: CREATE IMMEDIATE FUND AT FIRST DEATH — GROWS AT INTEREST — KEEP CONTRIBUTIONS TO IRREVOCABLE TRUST DOWN.

3.

4.

Items *2Da)* and *2Db)* were ledger statements which we had prepared to show two possible solutions to the second death problem. To the left, you will spot my instructions to Lori regarding which illustrations to prepare. You will also spot her handwriting correcting my request for minimum outlay to the correct computer terminology of "strip."

Points *3* and *4* were left vacant to accommodate any new items which arose.

At the bottom there is the legend, "1+5+1" which is my shorthand for one orginal, five photos, and one acetate. This interview was to be done with six people present and I was going to use the overhead projector. The extra copies could be handled in one of two ways. I could have handed them out and asked everyone to follow along on the overhead machine, or I could have used the machine without passing out the copies to the participants. I allowed myself the option of waiting to see how the meeting developed. As it turned out, I did not pass out the agendas; I only used the overhead and after the meeting gave one copy to the corporation, one to the lawyer, and one to one of the accountants.

Incidentally, there were a couple of sales completed and the agenda and layout worked successfully. All parties participated and it was a board meeting type of interview instead of just a sale with the agent guiding all the discussion.

Illustration 9-2 is the finished product of the handwritten copy we have just studied as Illustration 9-1. You can compare the two sheets and see the final result of adding and deleting items.

The previous agenda, which we just examined, was rather complicated. It took into account many facets of estate and business planning, relations with other advisors, and presentations of insurance plans. It was a good place to start because it was such a busy worksheet and it demonstrated the time which goes into planning a complex meeting. Illustration 9-3 should now appear to you as a rather simple one to further simplify the intention of simplification.

The purpose of this interview was to touch up the final details of an annual pension review for the "EM DISTRIBUTORS, INC." employees retirement plan. I was meeting with only one of the trustees who was the one who did all of the dealings for the plan. There were two trustees listed in the plan document but this person was the one who had the power to act. The other corporate head concerned himself with other matters of the company.

The annual plan date was July 15th, and all the work for increases of insurance, terminations of departed employees, and additions of new participants had already been done. This meeting was for the side investment fund deposit, and dealing with all the special areas which arose after the individual meetings had been held with the employees. This employer had been a client for over fifteen years and among the pension plan, individual estate planning for many of the principal owners and key executives, and the business planning, there were always considerable details to be done in the two or three months following the annual trust date.

Through the years, we had used two insurance companies as the carriers. Items *1.* and *2.* referred to the final work which had to be done for the insurance portion of the plan. By choice of the employer the insurance policies were held in the vault of the insurance company and certificates were given to each participant each year. Item *1A.* was a reminder to me to deliver the new updated annual certificates to the trustee with whom I was now meeting. Item *1B.* was a surrender check I was delivering for employees G and K who were terminated and had no vested interest in the plan. Therefore, the entire check was to be deposited back into this defined contribution plan. I could have elaborated further by putting the amount of the check in the agenda. Point *1C.* was for the removal of the insurance certificates of these two employees from the file folder the trustees kept for all records. I wanted to see him destroy these sheets so I knew there would be no confusion in later years. This entire Item *1.* was for the purpose of housekeeping on the policies of Connecticut Mutual.

Item *2.* had to do with the policies of insurance company "D." This company had the practice of producing a new policy and delivering it to the trustees each year. The object was the same as in Item 1. but here I had to physically pick up the policies for employees G and L.

Item *3.* involved a meeting which employee V had requested when I saw him at his annual review. He was a very high income earner as a salesman for this corporation. His attorney had told him it may be to his advantage to offer his services to the corporation as a manufacturer's representative for his own corporation. Thus far, it was against the practices of the employer to deal with reps from outside manufacturers. When I met with V, he told me he wanted to incorporate and asked me what would happen to his interest in this corporate pension plan. He also wanted to know how we could tie it into a plan which he would establish for his own corporation. This was a subject I would certainly not comment upon while I was dealing with V. My first employer was EM Distributors and that was the basis upon which I was meeting with V, as an employee.

Therefore, when V started to question me regarding the advisability of his incorporating and setting up his own plan, I sensed this was a discussion he already had had with his employer. I could also see myself getting into all kinds of difficulties by offering my advice so, I ducked all the questions and told him the truth. I said what he desired was possible but it was certainly a matter of practice and policy he would have to discuss with his employer before I could meet with him about the benefits to both parties in such a move. Incidentally, it would have been to his advantage to be his own corporation but his primary customer would have been this very company and, therefore, he really had to abide by their decision and that would, obviously, be what benefited the company the most.

My objective in reporting this to the employer was to protect myself with a revelation of all the details which had occurred during the employee meetings I had conducted. I especially wanted to be the first to let the employer know all the tiniest details of my discussion with V. I would not have known what he would have reported back to me after he had discussions of his own with the employer. By revealing the facts of my meeting with V back to the corporation I let it be known who was my primary employer in this transaction. I gave the full, honest version of what was discussed without opinion and without bias. The corporation could do what it wanted with the information. This was not a breach of confidence with V because I had told him it might be to his benefit to deal as a separate entity with his employers and I would discuss it with them. I also told him I would not offer advice to him without having both sides present at a meeting which they would call for the purpose of putting this whole issue on the table for a mutually beneficial negotiation. This agenda was dated 1980 but, up to now, the status of all the salesmen of this company has not changed. For the company's own purposes it prefers to deal with these people as employees.

Item *4A.* had to do with the side fund deposit which had to be made at this time; it amounted to $50,616.60. Item *4B.* asked about where the investment money would go. Thus far, in this plan, the investments had been done in bank trust departments and mutual funds. In asking the question, I was inviting the trustee to speak regarding his experience. I wanted to get him to put part of the existing fund, and this new deposit, into an

Illustration 9-3

EM DISTRIBUTORS, INC.

AGENDA — SEPTEMBER 26, 1980

1. CONNECTICUT MUTUAL LIFE
   A. NEW CERTIFICATES
   B. TERMINATION CHECK — G & K
   C. DESTROY G & K CERTIFICATES
2. D LIFE
   A. PICK UP G & L POLICIES
3. V MEETING
4. SIDE FUND CONTRIBUTION
   A. $50,616.60
   B. INVESTMENT VEHICLE?
5. KEY MAN INSURANCE
   A. WITH OR WITHOUT EQUITY?
6. M L
7. H W
8.
9.
10. REFERRALS

annuity vehicle. My simple question, "INVESTMENT VEHICLE?" could have been an elaborate presentation unto itself but this simple little question accomplished just as much. In addition, it was handled routinely as a part of the agenda.

Item *5A.* was really out of place in this agenda since it had to do with conversion of some term insurance on the president of the company. It probably should have been a separate agenda for the company rather than the trust, or possibly a separate listing after all the pension business. However, since it was the only outside item I had to discuss with this decision maker I put it in this spot. Upon looking at it now, I think it is out of place but it will exemplify the effectiveness of a working agenda which handles all matters as a routine of an effective business meeting. I had along a two column illustration which showed the present term premium listed as "WITHOUT EQUITY" in one of the columns and a whole life premium column listed as "WITH EQUITY." I'm happy to say we made the conversion.

Points *6.* and *7.* had to do with two very minor discussions I had with other employees, so I placed them last on the agenda. These were items which could have been skipped altogether but they were a nice way of exiting from the tougher stuff we had just completed. I conveyed this attitude when we got to these items by saying, "Items six and seven are really nothing earth shattering but. . . ." By putting these small items into the pension review agenda, the employer felt he was still on top of the plan even though I had had meetings with employees when he was not present.

Items *8.* and *9.* were left vacant so we could add new things which he might have brought up. This way, we would mark them down and get to them in order. The interview would be more like a boardroom type of dialogue and not a monologue delivered by me. Remember, this is one of the purposes of the agenda; to get both parties involved.

Item *10.* is the lifeblood of our business and I hadn't had any referrals from this corporation in a longtime. They were growing and had dealings with many other companies I wanted to meet. I placed the word "REFERRALS" right there in all it's blatancy so it would be seen early and long, in addition to being a reminder for me to ask for names.

Illustration 9-4 is an interesting agenda because it combines both a personal interview with a corporate one. At the top you will see listed the name of the corporation, "B. . . F," the word "agenda," and the date, "January 20, 1983."

The first section deals with the personal policies of one of the principals of the firms, M.R. and it is listed as "M________R-PERSONAL." Item *1.* was a summary of his policies which had just been reviewed and updated. Item *2.* was a refund check from Connecticut Mutual. We had just converted one term policy and there was an amount of $156.51 due him in the process.

Item *3.* was a reminder to him to write me a check for $217.70. This was an amount I had advanced him in making the change from the previous term policy. Item *4.* was as straightforward as it could be—I was asking for referrals.

Items *4.* and *5.* do seem to be a little out of sequence and probably should have been reversed. I should have explained to him the quarterly premium amount before I got to the point about referrals. I don't remember why I did it this way but, upon looking at it now, I probably just goofed. In looking over these five items, you will observe it does a number of things: it gets all the detail work done in a quick, orderly fashion; it allows me to put all of it in the agenda so nothing is forgotten and; it outlines all of it simply so we can flow smoothly, which was important because there was a lot to cover under the corporate agenda.

Items *6.* and *7.* were left blank for any issues which might have been brought up by the client. There were none.

The second section of the agenda had to do with one of the corporations owned by this one person along with two other people. I was dealing with M.R. because he had the power to act for the others and this was just a matter of delivering some new policies which had been applied for a few months earlier. I differentiated the fact we were now under the corporate section by the title "B____________________G—CORPORATE."

Item *1.* was a display of all the corporate policies on a summary sheet which he and I reviewed. Item *2.* showed the amounts of premiums due that we just had increased for the two shareholders. Their initials are shown as "J.B." and "R.F." along with the amounts of premiums for the two of them. I showed the total of $2,226.00 and the instruction to make the check payable to Connecticut Mutual. He immediately called out from behind his desk through the open door, "Carol, make out a check to Connecticut Mutual for $2,226.00." This is typical of the result an agenda

Illustration 9-4

B F
AGENDA
JANUARY 20, 1983

M R — PERSONAL

1. Summary of Policies
2. Refund from Connecticut Mutual — $156.51
3. Check made payable to Burt Meisel — $217.70
4. Referrals
5. Mode — Quarterly — $222.19
6.
7.

B G — CORPORATE

1. Summary of Policies
2. Premiums Due: J B $1,181.00
   R F $1,045.00
   Total: $2,226.00 Annual
   Payable to Connecticut Mutual
3. Sign Amendment for R F
4.
5.
6. Deliver Policies
7.
8.

brings; the clients want to complete their part in an efficient fashion as we go through these items. He could have waited for the whole interview to be completed before he did his part, but this might have confused things so he acted on each point as it arose. This kept his mind on track and clear between the personal and business items. The handwritten "R" next to the premium total was some scratching of mine indicating from which corporation the check was to come. They had more than one company and this check had to come from "R."

Item *3.* required the signature of R.F. Apparently, I did something wrong or the home office manufactured a reason for some more paperwork because we needed this amendment form which I now requested. He was not in the office so it had to be left with an envelope made out to me to be mailed when he returned.

Items *4a)* and *4b)* had to do with some paperwork for assignments which had to be made between individuals and corporations. Here is where the mother's note system of agendas is so important to me. It would be simple to confuse the amount of paperwork I had on this case. By using the agenda system and placing the various forms in a file folder in the order I was to use them, I did not forget any nor confuse any. They were all noted at my office with the initials of the individuals who had to sign and the corporation from which they came. This was because each of the individuals may have had different positions in the different companies. On the appointment, the clients just had to sign where and how indicated.

Items *5.* and *5a)* had to do with the legal framework change which had just occurred which necessitated this need for additional insurance. For my own purposes, I wanted to verify that all the title work was correct in accordance with the agreements which were in force, along with the new one which had just been drawn. I did not yet have a copy of the new one so this note was my reminder to get one, either at this meeting or to call the attorney and have one sent.

Item *6.* just reminds me to leave the policies and not forget and take them back with me, which I have done on occasion. I find since I have used the agenda system, I have made fewer of the dumb mistakes that I have made in the past. I just do all the brainstorming in my office, mark it down, and follow the instructions on the agenda once I get to the meeting. It is important to do it this way since so much activity goes on in a business meeting. The client has his or her agenda, too. Most times it is not written down in an orderly fashion and he or she just springs the details on us as they appear in their minds. For this reason I always include blank items, which show up here as items *7.* and *8.*

This meeting took about an hour to complete. It could have been done in half the time if we would have stuck directly to the agenda, but we all know that never happens. There are other things the client wishes to discuss or there are interruptions of one kind or another. The meeting would most likely have taken two hours if there were no agenda. If I did not have all these items marked down on one piece of paper, I probably would have forgotten something. In this appointment, we spoke of two corporations and one personal estate. In addition, he shared with me the thought of opening another business outside of Michigan and outlined what the problems of that venture now entailed.

No matter how the conversation twisted and turned, I was always able to get back on track because of the agenda. Before the interview got too far, there were papers all over my client's desk but we always got one matter cleared up and returned to the agenda for the next step. I was happier and the client was happier to be organized. As I finished, I reminded him to three-hole punch this sheet and put it into the corporate minute book. There would be no way for him to recall all the things which went on at this meeting. By putting the sheet in the minute book, it would be there for the other advisors to use when necessary, or they could call me and I could refer to my copy while they look at theirs.

10

Why Don't They Say What They Mean?

The art of answering objections depends upon just that: answering the objection. That sounds like a bit of a riddle but analyze the sentence carefully which, in and of itself, relates to the thought I am trying to convey. People don't say what they mean, generally, and they don't always give us the true objection the first time they say something with regard to our propositions. Too often, we never really get the true hesitancies to a sales presentation. If we can't answer the real objection, anything else is a waste of time and effort. It is the skill of a good salesperson which allows him or her to get to the honest reason for not proceeding, which ultimately results in greater sales and satisfaction for both the client and the agent.

I used to joke with my kids by telling them I could play any children's game in the world as long as all the players understood English. It did not matter if the game required special skill, dexterity, or specialized knowledge. Rules made no difference; equipment mattered not. I could play and compete and be fully involved whether it was a girl's game or a boys' game. Even if it was a game which used certain running, jumping, or other athletic skills which I may not have had, I could play and be an integral part of the competition. This applied to inside games, outside games, table games, or anything else.

I contend anyone in the world can join in a kid's game and be a vital member even if they don't know the rules of the game. All one has to know is four key phrases which apply to every game children play. These lines are: 1) "I quit;" 2) "You cheat;" 3) "I'm gonna tell" and; 4) "That's not fair." If it is a game which involves equipment there is another important line such as, "Gimme my bat, I'm going home." Just listen to your kids and their friends play a game and, within two minutes, you will hear one of these trivial non-truisms shouted. Stick around long enough and you will hear all of them. If it does get to the point where all of them are used, it was a successful game. These people were close friends who stuck together for long periods through thick and thin.

I observed these ploys whenever kids got together. When they were spoken, they did not stop or impede the game in any way even though the threat was that one was going to leave, or the other was a lying, cheating villain of some sort. That should have broken up the action, but it never did. It was part of the game to object to something which happened or to dispel the other's good fortune or skill by saying one of these required quotes. Most often, they were not even heard or no one realized they were being said. The game never slowed and the slander may have even added a sense of keener competition to the real intention of the jousting.

They didn't mean it when they said one of these negatives. Yet, it was the way the game was played and, by saying it, the speaker let it be known some action or positive gain of the offensive player did not go unnoticed. The action in kids games was always spirited and lively. Unlike the game show contestant on TV where even the legitimate competition has a prepared, staged atmosphere, these kids were intense. They went at the game viciously. When one set was done, another was started immediately. Only one thing could interrupt a game and it wasn't the saying of one of these slanders or any other more inventive one which was hurled. The only thing that could stop a game was mother's call for mealtime. That was the true objection. Mother had better have meant it, too, otherwise they knew how far they could extend the time before the message was serious. It could have been the first call or the second or possibly more, but they knew when they got to the real stuff.

Kid's were always eager to tell the truth; or their version of it, as long as it did not reflect badly on them. If it involved the others let the consequences fall where they may; the truth will win out. I could always catch up on the activities of my children with one key phrase. If I was not present for a while and I wanted to know everything that went on while they were on their own, I could use this one quip and be caught up within thirty seconds about every little detail which had transpired since I was away. Upon entering the room or yard where they had been playing, all I had to say was, "I saw that."

Then, all the small and large complaints on the others, all the imagined malignments and, all the jealousies came spewing out. They all started to talk at once: "She took my. . .," "She spilled the. . .," "He said. . .," "Mother told me I could . . .," "I didn't . . .," et cetera to include any number of "fill in the dots" cryptograms on what someone else had done. My jobs were to listen fast and carefully, and to piece in one's complaint as compared to the other's. They all talked at once and it didn't take long for me to catch up on all the activities of this encounter and others past.

The fact was I didn't see anything but just said, "I saw that." Parents or other authoritarians have to act as interpreters or referees when the communication is not clear or comes as mixed signals from diverse directions. The game of business is not too much different from the games of kids or the game of life, in general. The objections are a part of the communication process. Many of the agendas and one page proposals I have shared in this book are designed to either bring forth intended, expected objections or to answer the obvious objections before they start. Frequently, on my speaking engagements, I will ask if there are any questions after showing some of the illustrations. It is rare I get a question. I suppose some of it is the intimidation factor of speaking forth in large audiences, but I always ask again, "Any questions?" When there are none, which is most of the time, I thank the audience for not having any and tell them I take that as a compliment because that is what the illustrations are designed to do.

Either in the usual one-on-one interview or in a business boardroom type interview the objecting process is part of the sales process. This is, once again, part of life and it is part of what is called "salesmanship" and "prospectship." All of us do it; even salespeople become the objectors when they are the buyers. This happens even when the purchase is a foregone conclusion that has taken place in the mind before the actual process. How many of you have shopped cars until you know exactly what you want and the decision has been made in your brain, but all that remains is to sign the papers? Even then, have you ever asked just one more question as to the gas mileage or some other trivial matter which wouldn't dissuade you from buying, no matter what the answer? The salesperson recognizes the buying signals, compliments you on a brilliant question and gives you just the answer you wanted to hear. Just a little soothing but it puts you in the buying seat instead of the sold seat. You bought but you were not sold.

I have gone into men's clothing stores knowing precisely what I wanted to buy. I have given the clerk the order stating carefully the item, size, and color, having it on and loving it, asking a question as to whether or not it will show much lint, or if this item is a popular seller. It's natural to object as buyers even if we have to plant a leading question. No one likes the feeling of having been sold. It is far better to consider one's self as a discerning purchaser.

Therefore, objecting in some cases is just questing for more information. It is important we, as salespeople, recognize the difference between a true and serious objection, and a question which is legitimately asking for more clarification. So why don't they say what they mean? And further to the point, in our business, why are they so mean? Usually, the true objection, when it finally comes, is a legitimate concern that evokes a sincere answer which will dissolve the deterrent to proceeding. Or, as a friend of mine once said to a really silly objection on a large business case, "Why do you make me work so hard to do you so much good?"

Some of the objections we get are downright nasty. Some of those we hear are almost insulting to the product, companies and the agents. I wouldn't have the nerve to say some of the things I hear about our product to someone else in reference to his or her industry. I don't have the gall to look a stockbroker or banker in the eye and say, "Your business is nothing but a racket." I have heard that about our profession, spoken vociferously by persons I wouldn't have believed had all that venom in their stomachs.

It is natural to object to new ideas which make people change long-standing patterns to adopt something new. I would rather have an interview with someone who is paying thousands of dollars in premiums as opposed to someone who has no insurance. It would appear the non-insured would more readily be a candidate as contrasted with the one who has considerable coverage for which he or she is already paying. Not so, for the following reason. The prospect who is presently paying premiums made the wise decision years before to own some life insurance. The process now is merely to touch it up so it is more realistic with current needs. The decision to go from $500 a month in premiums to $600 a month is easier than going from $0 to $10 per month. In the one case there already exists a budgetary item known as "premiums." In the other the decision is whether or not to create a new category. That does take some thinking and does make for a tougher interview.

In the instance of the owner of existing insurance, the decision is based directly on needs. There is no surprise that there will be something to pay in order to get something new. In the situation of the non-owner, there is a completely foreign item which is being presented. Insurance was not a part of the previous jargon. This brings to my mind the question of why anyone in their right mind would disagree with the notion of creating something large out of something which did not earlier exist. So why do they object? Why doesn't everyone say "yes" all the time? If this line of thinking is correct, the only objection which would hold any validity would be, "I can't afford it," spoken by the prospect who honestly means it.

I have adopted some theories on why people object. I must admit, these are not original with me. I heard them from a speaker at an MDRT meeting. He said intended insureds object for only three legitimate reasons. There are no others and anything else falls in the family of one of these three main stalls:

1) it is postponable;
2) it is intangible;
3) it is for the benefit of someone else.

The only one of these which I have ever heard spoken exactly as stated about is the intangible objection. There are many, many objections which we have heard through the years. There are very few which I have never heard before. It is rare someone surprises me with a new one or one which I could not answer with some stock rebuttal. Every retort to which I have ever listened falls into one of these sections. They come in all varieties but, just like the automobile industry in the United States, we are dominated by the big three.

IT IS POSTPONABLE

This one comes in all flavors from the simple, "See me later," to the exotic ones such as, "After tax season" or, "Let me see if I get a bonus and how much it is." Others in this segment are, "See me after the first of the year," (substitute Christmas, Thanksgiving, Labor Day, vacation, or any of the other holidays negotiated by any strong major labor union, tax season, my son's Bar Mitzvah, my daughter's first communion, finals, my store's sale, and so forth.)

Most of these are purely and simply stalls. They weren't meant to be serious and are just a test of the agent to see just how intent he or she is about the offer just made. They make about as much reasonable sense as a child saying to its mother, "I'll make my bed later." If mama doesn't follow through, it will never be made. And why will it be easier to make later than it is now? One of the best answers I ever heard came from a cartoon; it was to a request for a delayed payment. It showed a cashier behind the cage in a flop-house responding to a bum who had asked for a waiver of that night's fifty cent fee. The balloon in the comic said, "If you can't pay me fifty cents tonight, what would make me believe you can pay me a dollar tomorrow?"

There are lots of answers to the postponable objection, such as the simple agreement of seeing the person after their designated later date. You say, "Fine, let's make the time right now. We'll put it in our calendars and I will send you a reminder card just before the meeting." If the objection was genuine, they will agree with you and make the date. If not, they will have to make another stab at negativism, and you will be getting closer to the real objection. Another simple response is to simply agree and state you will mark your records and call at the appointed time.

More complicated answers might entail the questioning method of repeating the objection and asking a further question such as, "I don't mind calling you after the first of the year. That really is no problem for me to mark my records. But, tell me, seriously, what can happen to enhance the proposal between now and then? You're not going to get any younger, you're healthy now so that can't improve any more, the return to you will not be larger by waiting, and the annual outlay will not be any less. There really is no good reason to delay. This is a good thing for you to do; let's get started."

To some people the arranging of life insurance is sincerely a postponable thing. It is hard to realize, or even bring to mind, the possibility of dying and not being here to carry on. It is not a pleasant thought, at best. It is tough to think of one day becoming an angel. So we, as salespeople, try to soften the dismal thoughts by focusing on the cash values in the future. However, most people don't want to think about growing older. Yet the question I ask is, "Are you still measuring your future earnings and career in decades or in months?" I have found that to be a heavy question. It sure makes one think about the time already wasted by not having adequate protection for the survivors. Incidentally, I frequently refer to the future in months rather than years. It does seem 240 months is a shorter time than 20 years. A favorite line of mine, when asking for an appointment, is to ask for a sixty-minute meeting. Sixty minutes is shorter than an hour, isn't it?

The right words, actions, or listening skills are powerful tools. Too much anxiety about being the next one to speak shows through. The other party can tell if you are intently listening and they will appreciate it more than if they sense you are abiding their conversation only until you can jump in. Sixty minutes are certainly no longer than one hour; they are equal in elapsed time but by mentioning minutes rather than hours emphasis and value is put on even the smallest unit. When this happens, the thought processes open up with a desire to hear more innovative ideas.

One thing I do to get service people to appreciate rather than expect tips is to use the Susan B. Anthony silver dollars. As you know, they closely resemble quarters and there could easily be confusion between the two. When travelling, I first have someone stop at the bank for me and get ten of them. They are bulky to carry and ten single paper dollars would be easier to handle, but I want the coin dollars to create a difference in service and appreciation. When you tip a baggage handler with paper they hardly look at it. The hand is automatically out and it gobbles up the paper with little effort. Something is expected and when it is given, it disappears robot-like into a pocket. If you give one bill, the person knows automatically it was a one; they know the service wasn't worth a five or a ten dollar tip so they do mental arithmetic on the day's take without even seeing what you presented. If you give two bills, they realize more emphatically these are not five's or ten's and you may get a little louder, "Thank you." However, in most cases, it is still perfunctory.

An amusing thing happens when I tip with the coin dollars. I may hand a skycap two of these coins and the first look on his face is one of slight disdain or surprise and, maybe, even a little disgust with this customer. But then they look at the coins to verify they were only given fifty cents to do the chore. They may be getting ready for a full-blown insult or leer but they see there is something different about these quarters. When they realize they were given two dollars, which is no gigantic tip, (maybe only in the right range) they feel a lot better. However, the thought processes went in a few directions before it got back to the fact this is money, this is a good amount but, most importantly, it could have been fifty cents and not two dollars. Then, there has to be a feeling of appreciation. If it is not one of thanks for receiving a tip which is universally expected, it is one of getting the higher amount; it could have been worse. I sense I get a little better service when I make my service people cogitate about the fact I didn't have to give at all.

Little, inconsequential actions like that can make people think about their own business just by slowing them down and breaking up the big picture into smaller parts. The same thing is true in the art of interviewing. We sometimes become too automated in our responses. They are quick, predictable, and sometimes without feeling. The way around all of that is sensitive listening and sensible and sincere responding. Early in the business we all studied the art of answering objections. Usually the supervisor spent time with us rehearsing and role playing the part of a consumer. There may be key words or families of words which evoke certain responses. I remember the automatic for, "I can't afford it," was "But can you afford to be without it?" It's true and it's meaningful but not if it is thrown out as a rebound with the intent of "take that; now I gottcha!"

One of the reasons buying and owning life insurance is postponable is the fact that it is voluntary. It is true; it is postponable, forever, if so desired. But somebody has to pay something someday. If the responsible party does not pay sufficient premiums to provide the desired funds for his dependents, they will pay the full dollars by doing without. There is the law of physics which states matter can neither be created nor destroyed. I don't know if that applies to the principles of life insurance. Technically, it does since life insurance is money and money is matter. There is nothing new created when a life insurance policy flowers to full maturity either late in its being or early.

The dollars came from somewhere. They were not created by magic. It came from the pool of money created by the payment of premiums by many, many policyowners. The payment of a claim was merely the result of spreading the risk to many so the loss to the individual was not great. The loss spoken of here was not the death but the disappearance of earnings. The risk to the individual, if insured, were the premiums paid. If uninsured, it was the whole amount which the survivors will forego, and sometimes that is immeasurable. There is no way of knowing what might have been. The oil filter commercial on TV sums it up very well when it shows the sacrifice of the price of a filter or the loss of the whole engine. The same guy does the work; either he sells the customer the filter or he repairs the engine. And he woefully says, "Pay me now or pay me later."

The premiums will be paid sometime so, "See me later" may be a pitifully prophetic statement. Too often life insurance people have a tough time speaking to their own relatives. There is that feeling of obligation that exists which makes it uncomfortable for both the agent and the prospect. Actually, the obligation should be for the agent to work twice as hard because this is someone who is related by blood and, in this case, he or she is his brother's keeper. If you doubt me, think ahead or recall from memory the case of a relative dying underinsured while the relative agent is known as a successful salesperson in the community. People will talk and they ain't being complimentary.

I know of one case where a successful agent, while early in his career, approached his in-laws about retirement planning policies. For whatever the reason, he was rebuffed and rather embarrassingly so. When the father-in-law died, it was this agent who did all the necessary probate and legal running. The estate consisted primarily of a home, which was paid for, a small amount of cash and a minimal amount of life insurance. The money is not sufficient to provide a full income to the mother-in-law so the agent and his wife help out financially, as needed. Now who's paying the premium?

Answering the objections can happen any time in the sales and, eventual, servicing relationship. The three basic times are the initial phone or personal solicitation call, the actual interview, or the policy delivery. It has been both my experience and observation that the toughest time of objection comes at the initial approach, the time of making the appointment. Most of the answers or ideas in this chapter are directed to that time of initial contact. I realize many agents will have difficulty in closing the sale on the actual interview. This takes into account my notion that the close starts at the open. Every contact from word one is part of the closing process. The actual final words asking a prospect to take action on an interview is called the close but that only refers to the moment of climax.

For me, and in my observations, the hardest part of selling was always the first voice-to-voice contact. Further, for me, that was the telephone. I believe the greatest percentage of agents use the phone as the preeminent method of making appointments. Of course, face-to-face cold calling is more effective once the actual confrontation occurs, but for all the reasons of efficiency of time and volume of contacts, the phone wins out as the prime medium of initial contact. In the earlier chapters of the book I concentrated on agendas and proposals which are designed to close the sale. In those, I attempt to plant seeds for objections and the basis for questions with answers already printed in the proposals. For instance, in the "Retail-Wholesale" interview, I placed all the objections I ever heard to buying business insurance in two columns.

Therefore, to my way of thinking, the biggest objection and the easiest time to invoke "See me later" is on the telephone at the first contact. Of course, it is a common objection even after something has been presented, but it is easy to postpone or fight off a meeting with "See me later" if one has never seen the caller before. To summarize this section on the postponable beliefs of our prospects, accept it as the nature of the romance process of selling and prepare yourself for it. A good response for nearly all kinds of objections (and it fits well in this section about delays) is one taught by Jim Jacobs, CLU, of the Detroit area. He responds to most objections by listening carefully to what is being said, thereby showing a sense of credence and not just one of sales banter. He answers sincerely and quietly, "I know how you feel. Many people have felt that way. But let me tell you what we have found." He then goes on to answer the objection with whatever explanation he feels best fits the situation. He calls it "The Feel, Felt, Found" method. I have used it and it does convey more of the "counselor" selling method rather than the "salesperson" route.

IT IS INTANGIBLE

One way or another we hear this objection many times. I used to hear friends or other acquaintances tell me, "I couldn't sell insurance for anything, it's intangible." I never fully knew what that meant. I know technically "intangible" means that which can not be seen, touched, or felt. But I never could make the relationship between something intangible and something as potent as life insurance. With the insurance agreement the policyowner has a policy to hold and keep. It represents a stake in the future either for the owner through the cash value route, or a big part of tomorrow for the beneficiary via the proceeds.

I respond to this objection by saying a life insurance policy is about as intangible as a driver's license, a marriage certificate, a draft status card, the deed to a home, a bank book, a mortgage, or any other piece of paper which represents the ownership of a right or a future option or obligation.

I suppose the intangible idea comes primarily from the aspect of looking at a life insurance contract as an investment or savings vehicle. I admit, it doesn't give as much action as a stock or mutual fund which changes daily and takes careful tending so one is in command of the investment. However, that is the purpose of the product, to make a decision today which will weather the financial storms of tomorrow. Those decisions are all encompassed in our policies. They are meant to be different vehicles for different aspects of one's protection or investment goals. I have heard, "A life insurance policy is a lousy investment." In the hands of an astute investor, it is correct so I offer the argument, "I agree, most life insurance policies are lousy investments, but most investments are lousy protection." For our purposes here, we will not get into the aspects of the merits of term and permanent insurance; we have already had a large segment on that elsewhere in the book. For this discussion we will stay on the big picture of analyzing the three large categories of objections.

What about the individual who is not an investor and doesn't have the likelihood of ever having sufficient money to be one? In his or her case the life insurance premiums must be double duty dollars. There is no choice. For this person, and to some extent for the person with an investment portfolio, life insurance is a thankfully intangible product. Sometimes, it is best for all of us not to be able to get our hands on our investments. There are those items which are designed to be good both for the short run and the long-haul. Life insurance is one of those which can be put away and forgotten. In most instances, the only changes which are necessary in the future are additions to the program.

I tell advocates of the "intangible" opinion, Life insurance does something fairly well and that is investment. It guarantees a return of the principle promised. It does another thing very well and that is savings. It is there when it is needed. One more thing it does eminently well is that of protection. There isn't another financial instrument which can boast about all of that for the same dollar that is put away today and will be there for the future. Further, in some cases insurance is the best investment available for certain people. The "intangible" nature removes it from access to a bad investment track record. Indeed, I have had wealthy investors eagerly buy permanent insurance because it will "be there" in the future.

Think of the tangibility of a marriage certificate or a driver's license. In both cases, they are merely pieces of paper which permit certain lifestyles, which are still voluntary, but are recognized by society if the principal parties so subscribe. The driver's license has become one of the foremost articles of identification in the United States. It tells more about your ability to cash a check than your skill at driving. No one ever checks a marriage certificate; if you say you're married, you're married. The paper is only symbolic. Compare that with the tangibility a personal representative demands when he or she is administering an estate and holds the life insurance folder in his or her possession. That's tangible!!!

A house is a tangible asset; the mortgage paper is not. The same thing holds true for a policy; the paper is as tangible as the mortgage and the proceeds are as tangible as the house. True, you can live in the house and not the policy but you can live in what the policy will provide when it is called upon to do so. It will do what its function is when it has to. The two things are different assets designed to accomplish different living goals at different times.

Thc bank book is only paper which represents the deposits in the bank. A policy does the same job. No difference here.

I do have to agree that a life insurance policy is intangible in one respect. The fruition of the policy happens sometime in the future. It is so safe that it is dangerous. If the client or other well- or ill-intentioned individuals leave it alone, it will sit idly by and grow with an awesome power to fulfill the promise and expectation of the policyowner. Yet today, it is only a contract which lolls about offering the absolute safety and assurance for the future date that it has to be tangible. I can find no fault with that and I so relate that to the objection about intangibility.

When we get too emotional about objections, without trying to analyze exactly what was said, we can get off into areas which do not address the problem. They only invoke other thoughts bordering on having a good discussion, similar to arguing politics or religion. Sometimes objections are only spoken as rhymes which someone has heard before and hope will dissuade the agent from bringing them face-to-face with a decision. Often, they don't even mean what they say; they are just talking, pleading to us to "tell me more."

The objections about not being tangible, or the one about not believing in insurance, are not true. I can't think of any religion which bans life insurance. In fact, in the *Bible* in Genesis 41, reference is made to the seven bad years and the seven good years. That isn't the home offices as we know them or any of the other formal facets such as policies, actuaries, computers, premium notices, etc. But it is universal in one respect; it was life insurance in the form of seven pay life with seven year settlement options.

When the argument of not believing in insurance arises, I answer it as follows: "It isn't meant to be a religious denomination or a political tenet. It is a financial planning method used to create something where nothing existed before." I also use this answer, "Some people don't believe in banks either; let's talk about it some more."

I don't think life insurance is intangible but I suppose to some folks who do, it is the area of future gratification that bothers them and not one of being able to have the same feeling as getting behind the wheel of a new car and smelling the new leather. It is our job to convey the reasons why our product can do all the things anyone wants. So, the argument about intangibility is only saying, "Tell me more." Try to get to the real root objection which, most times, is just a matter of talking about the product until all the questions are satisfied. Hopefully, the prospect will realize all the values of the system and understand he or she can not do it alone.

IT IS FOR THE BENEFIT OF SOMEONE ELSE

To my mind, this is the most meaningful objection of all. It tells an awful lot about the character of the prospect. This is one where I listen carefully. Of course, it is never spoken in this fashion, although I have heard some gruff characters say something like, "I don't care what happens to anyone else after I die." If the speaker said that with any kind of conviction, I would believe him or her and leave the interview. Even if one does not mean that when it is spoken, those are damning words to say even in jest. I know that most objections are cosmetic and only mean, "Tell me more" but to be so blunt and forthright about dependents really takes a ton of chutzpah.

I think we have all heard the insurance planning of idiots which comes in the form of, "When I die she won't have any trouble finding another husband right away" or, "She's good looking, she'll probably marry someone and be better off than she is now." Years ago, I used to hear this fail-safe insurance planning which did not utilize the services of a company or a policy, "My wife has her teaching certificate and will go back to work if I die." Times change and the years march on. Even teachers with tenure are hanging on by their fingernails.

In 1958, which was my third year in the business, I sold a $5,000 permanent policy with a $20,000 mortgage rider to a young man. He was delighted with this much insurance for such a little premium. He told me his father was 52-years-old and there were still five children left at home, with the youngest being two. He felt his dad should have a policy of this nature so he called the father right then and I arranged an appointment.

Dennis, the son, had told his father he was paying $11 a month for his policy. The father, therefore, was shocked when his premium for the same plan came to $40 per month, let alone the fact that he would never develop the cash equity as would his son. He lectured me on the beauty of his group plan which provided $12,500 protection at no premium to him. I explained the difference of group insurance and the fact that it was only a condition of employment and was there at the whim of the employer. He asked me to quote various premiums for plans of $12,500. Mistakenly, I did. He really was tough and had me working numbers for him right out of the rate book. He scoffed at the idea of whole life and thought the premium for twenty pay life was ridiculously high.

He went back to his theme of the virtues of group insurance and, once again, I mentioned the fact that it was not portable and he had no control over it. He glowered at me and said, "Kid, the only way I'll ever lose that group insurance is if Hudson Motor Car goes out of business." They did later that year.

He called me and we set up an appointment. He was now a broken man because he could not find regular work. Times were slow in Detroit during 1958 and the few firms hiring sporadically were not looking for 52-year-old foremen. He was a different man and I liked him better when he was tougher. It was truly hard for him to commit to a $15 monthly premium to pay for the $18,000 decreasing term for mortgage purposes.

For the next two or three years, he had a terrible time finding regular work and the premium was often beyond the grace period. The insurance company required a health form in order to accept it. On occasion, rather than chase after the form, I paid the premium for him and he paid me back. A couple of years later, he died and the claim was sufficient to pay off the mortgage. Even so, his wife had a difficult time keeping the family together and some of the young children went to live with other relatives. It was a tragic story but one I often think about since it was one of my first death claims. It had a powerful impact on me.

That was one of the stories about the benefit for someone else. I wonder how many insurance people he kicked down the stairs through the years. He didn't want to pay premiums because that would affect him immediately. But his motive was the same as that of many people who are against starting insurance programs in sufficient amount; the theme is selfishness.

There are people who will buy a new car on the east side of the street and not drive it to the west side to talk to the car insurance agent. They will call ahead to find out if the new chariot is covered before risking a scratch on it. Heaven forbid a ding for a couple of hundred dollars. Yet if that person were killed in an accident while walking across that street, it is doubtful he or she would have had themselves as well protected as the new car. Which is worth more? I guess the answer is in the mind of the individual. However, the risk of the loss for the damage to a car is visible, it is here, it is now. Most importantly, it is "I" who will suffer.

That is the basis for the greed type objections which fall into this category of the benefit for someone else. Every thought and every objection will have the words "I" or "me" in it somewhere. It takes a lot of love and a lot of desire to truly do something for someone else without regard for yourself. I heard a TV minister give the the game plan for keeping yourself well. He said the secret for staying well physically, spiritually, and every other way, was to say a prayer for someone else. Truly, get into the spirit of wishing someone else well and the benefits will come to you multifold. The same thing is true about life insurance planning.

When the agent spends his or her time and efforts really thinking about the problems of the prospect, the objections seem to fold away. It is possible some of the objections we get are actually deserved because the prospect senses too much emphasis is being put on making a sale rather than solving the problems. We may feel, on occasions, that the prospect is handling the meeting in a childish fashion, objecting without any sound basis or logical reasoning. But at the same time he or she may feel the agent is playing children's games by not meaning what is being said. Remember when you were a child, it was possible to cancel anything which was said previously, or even to tell a lie, just by invoking the magic motions. Have you ever said the words, "Ha, ha, doesn't count, I had my fingers crossed"?

That seemed to work then. It conveyed one party was only fooling and what was said was not to be taken seriously. I sometimes feel the prospect is playing the same game with me when he or she uses some phony objection. It is childish but the stakes are much more severe. I suspect some of the silly objections which are tossed at agents are only done so because the prospect is feeling like a toy in a game of production. All of us can sense sincerity when it is about. By the same token, we can feel phoniness. It is natural to react to insincerity with suspicion so some of the objections we get are really testers asking us to convey some reassurance or to tell the prospect more. It is apparent the sham can come from either side of the interview desk.

When I realize the objection is a false one and is given without regard to the instant facts, I bring the interview back to a more serious basis by asking the following question, "Would you prefer I be honest or diplomatic?" I have never heard anyone say anything but "honest." Then I am free to tell it like it is. I have been invited to reveal my honest emotions. The other party can not be offended by whatever I say since they gave me license to say what I mean. The question is a potent one and brings excellent results.

Throwing objections is not an unusual process. It is natural in any social or business situation where one party is promoting something which is either a new product or a new idea. Think of the romance process. One party is dominant while the other resists. They both wish the same result but fear of the consequences stifles natural emotions. Eventually, when all the barriers are down and both parties do what they feel is in their mutual interests, they are both satisfied.

We see this in the courtship period, too. Can you think of any situations where people you know talk about the fact that one turned down the marriage proposals of the other a number of times before a union was consumated? Some of these marriages are the most solidly bonded partnerships, yet they started with an aura of distrust and doubt. The resister was saying to the other, "Tell me more." He or she wanted confirmation regarding this lifelong step. The same holds true when one buys a life insurance contract in favor of another person. It's designed to be a lifelong deal and all the aspects should be understood.

Some of these objections are sincerely felt and some are the romance process. In this section we are talking about buying insurance for the benefit of somebody else. For some people, it is a heavy undertaking to shed the natural feelings of greed and selfishness which are compounded with the factors of intangibility and postponability. Although I have mentioned three distinct categories of objections, I believe often times they cross over and all three interact with the same individual at the same time. It is possible to have a full gamut of procrastination going on in one's mind simultaneously.

If I ever had an interview where there were no objections or questions, it could only mean I did a bad interview. It is a natural thing to question and only means the prospect was paying some kind of attention. If there was no talking at all, I wouldn't know where I stood in relation to my presentation. We are trained to ask questions so that we evoke the thoughts of our counterparts. Dialogue is selling's language. A monologue is a lecture which is a completely different type of confrontation. In the lecture, an idea is being presented for consideration. In a sales interview, an idea is being presented with the intended objective of adoption.

If we adopt the position that objections are a part of the business which we must face all along the way, we should look forward to hearing them rather than not. If we're not getting them, we are just not doing the job right. They appear at every stop along the way from prospecting, to approaching, to closing. If we're not getting them, we're also not doing the other parts of selling. Remember, there is nothing personal in an objection. Also, keep in mind they come in every business, not only ours. And they come in every corner of life's daily activities, business or pleasure. Our posture is to be ready for them both in spirit and in wit. Spirit, so we are not thwarted when they come, and wit so we can answer the challenge when it is hurled.

To close out the chapter, let me try to tie in all three of the general sections which I have exposed: postponable, intangible and, for the benefit of somebody else. Let's see if I can do it in relation to someone else's service activities and in a business other than ours. I occasionally play in a Friday night poker game where the stakes are one and two dollars. The games we play call for split pots for the high and low hands. This means each pot has two winners and there is a division of the pot. Most of the fellows come armed with a supply of one dollar bills, plus whatever else they may have. I have seen that most pots had a mound of one dollar bills which took considerable time to split. When the splitting took place there was always a greedy grab for any five, ten, or twenty dollar bills which had been put in for change.

I reasoned to myself that organization was one of my strong points so the pots would go faster if the big number of ones could be facilitated. So, one Friday afternoon, I stopped in the bank and cashed a check asking for fifty $2 bills along with some other money. The answer I got from this young lady combined all three of the types of objections we have been studying in this chapter. She tried to postpone me, she told me the bills were intangible, and she showed me the benefit was for somebody else. She said to me, "I don't have any here. They're in the vault."

From that I gleaned she didn't want to go to the vault, therefore, she wanted to postpone the job or not do it at all. Her tone also indicated the bills were inferior to other denominations since she didn't even stock them. Her voice also had in it a slight disdain for me. For sure, she exuded it was for my benefit and not hers and her benefit would be better served if she didn't have to lockup her cage and go to the vault. I responded, "That's OK, I'll go to the vault." All of us in line and she knew that was not permissible but she surmised from my answer I was resolute in having my two's.

She did go to the vault and I did have my money as I wanted it. Interestingly, whenever I go to the bank and have another teller, the whole scene gets repeated and I have a few moments of fun watching it unfold. When our receptionist goes to the bank for me to get the Friday night booty, I tell her what to say when the resistance shows. She, too, is always amused by the show and surprised that it keeps happening.

After getting by the humor and analyzing it, I think my retort was a pretty good one and I'm proud of myself for coming up with one which smacks down the objections and gets the job done. But consider the tellers who keep saying it, and they do. They don't even realize they are conveying a mind set which they got early in the day, that of staying in certain comfortable surroundings (their wicket) and not having to lockup the cage to do special functions. They don't mean to convey not wanting to do the task for me as an individual; it's just an automatic feeling of, "No one else uses those things. Why does he need them?" The bills are legal tender and I think I have come up with a perfect utility for them. I believe the tellers are not thinking of my needs or their total functions at all.

Why don't they say what they mean? I hope I have presented some of the reasons they don't so that we can now sharpen our skills and say what we mean.

11

Don't Take It Personally

The theme of this book has been how to get the most out of your work. We started by talking about the numbers aspect of cultivating large amounts of names in order to cull those who will be clients. I demonstrated many aspects of my operation showing how I prepared and used various illustrations and agendas in order to put the right emphasis in the right spot. The goal of all of this is to minimize the loss ratio of time and effort. Still, we have to strike out some time. We have to have certain unexplainable, goofy situations which occur from time to time. If not, we haven't been exposing ourselves enough times in order to establish a field from which to make our selections as to who will be clients and who will not.

They don't all close and we don't want all of them to close; it's an impossibility. If an agent were giving away policies, he or she could not have a 100 percent efficiency rate. Someone out there couldn't pass the physical or someone else would not "believe" in the product or another would be suspicious of anything that is sold by soliciting salespeople. All the things, events, objections or other stumbling blocks which we encounter in the daily pursuit of our business would come into play even if no premium were required. The percentages would change drastically but there would still be hurdles. One of the first percentages to change would be the commission rate.

Another factor that would change would be the rejection rate. It would decelerate drastically, but it would not be zero. There will always be those who, for their own reasons, will say "no." I suppose that is a good thing; it is what keeps us sharp for the real creative and challenging part of this business. So, the immutable facts are certain people will say "yes" and certain people will say "no." Sometimes, the "yes's" come in the most surprising places and, sometimes, the "no's" come from quarters which were completely unexpected.

The rejection comes with the territory and the rate book or the computer disc. There will always be rejection. The real question is how it affects us. If we take all of it as a personal rebuttal, we are bound to become downtrodden. It will show up in the sales columns and, more importantly, in our general demeanor and well-being. We know that many of those who leave the business do so because they did not handle it like a business but more like a personal mission. In some respects, it is a mission but it is not a personal one. Each of us lends our own personal flavor to the ways in which we operate, but that is a business side of us and not our personal selves.

One of the prime ways of minimizing the devastating effects of rejection is to refine the basis on which you approach prospects. I'll relate a story which I heard many years ago which, although not directly related to insurance, will pave the way for the points I want to make about getting nearer to the prospect earlier.

A professor who was a noted lecturer and public speaker was asked to address the graduating class at his alma mater. He was known as one of the most gifted extemporaneous speakers in the world and this is what the sponsoring committee wanted; a speech which was uplifting for the young graduates while, at the same time, not a sermon. It was anticipated he could get the feel of the personality of this particular class and send them forward from their years of study with eager, open minds.

He accepted the date willingly and made the proper notation in his schedule. About a week after the invitation and confirmation were made, he received a phone call from one of the committee members asking about the subject of his talk. The professor explained he never prepared a speech in advance and that is what made his style fresh and vibrant. The committeeperson appreciated his position and said they did not want the speech, only the title so it could be advertised in the commencement program. The professor understood but said he had no thoughts on the matter at that time and, since graduation was six months off, there was time to do the printing. He suggested the caller check back in a month.

When the follow-up phone call came, the professor still did not have a clue as to what the subject or title would be so he asked for another month to think about it. Dutifully, the call came on time. Still having no idea of what his talk would engender, he explained that was not unusual for him since he was strictly an "off-the-cuff" person. He suggested they go to press without a title and felt assured his name would be sufficient to gather deep interest and attention. There was no more time before the printing deadline so that is how it stood.

The programs were printed and the day came closer. The committee, just out of nervousness and nosiness, now wanted to know the subject or at least an inkling of what might be said. The committee chairman made a call to the professor and the response was the same as to the other calls; he simply had nothing in mind yet. But, not to worry; that was his usual format.

The big day came and dawned beautifully sunny. The professor was in town and had been housed the night before at the dean's residence. He had been regaled along with other dignitaries at fancy meals and on special tours. During these, he was asked about his subject and he answered he would not know until the next day, which was the day of commencement. In the morning, the dean himself asked about the subject and the professor responded he did not yet know. At this late date, everyone took this to mean he had a blockbuster of a subject and did not want any chance of having it leaked to the press or the audience.

On the contrary, what was really happening was that he had nothing in mind. He was worried; this had never occurred to him before. Usually, by this late hour, he had a firm outline in his thinking process. Two days back he had put his mind to this speech which he wanted to be his best in history. Nothing would come and he started to fret to himself, without revealing it to his wife or any other associates.

Now the moment was here. He was shown to a dressing room along with the other dignitaries who suited up in caps and gowns and relaxed before the call to the procession. One of the other honorees who knew the professor well asked what the subject would be; he was informed there was none, yet. This was a fact and, inwardly, the professor was genuinely worried. The call came and they fell into ranks. The pomp and circumstance took hold and already there was a special aura about the whole ceremony.

Now our professor was in deep trouble. This was the closest to a speech he had ever come without knowing what he would say. He felt nervous and dizzy. He wrestled with himself but his thoughts were thwarted. The procession started and he was marching but there was no clue as to what would be said; in fact, he was so woozy, he was even worried he might not be able to make it to the podium. They marched down the hall and right in front of them was the entrance to the large auditorium that was filled with graduates, faculty, families, and friends. There were aides everywhere and, normally, this would have been a pleasant walk because of all the first-class treatment accorded.

They were going through the double, retractable doors to the hall when the door attendant turned to greet someone and let the door slip just as the professor was about to enter. It slammed shut in front of him and everyone was startled for an instant. There it was shutting him out just like his thoughts regarding a subject. He was now facing a closed door with just the word "PUSH" in big, black letters staring him in the face. And in that little tick of time, the subject came to him. It was now clear what he would say and in the computer circuitry of his brain the whole speech took form and was a completed text.

The door was reopened and it was a new day for him. What had been a time of frustration and uncertainty was now reborn and as clear as it could be. He would talk about that one word "push" but he would never say it. He would refer to "drive, incentive, stick-to-itiveness, gumption, goals, motivation, activity, power, purpose, guts, fortitude, depth, profundity" and many other words referring to "push" but he would never say the word itself. He would tease and play with his audience. He would bring them to the edge of the word but he would not reveal it. He would have them guessing and he would have them participating in the speech by trying to find the solution as to what the word might be. All the while he would impart the message of going out into the real world with all the energy and drive which was needed to succeed. He would charge up this crowd like they had never been before.

He succeeded. They were with him. They shouted out their thoughts on the word. They participated in the talk. It was inspiring as a church service. He brought himself and the listeners to a fever pitch. The board was delighted. They had what they wanted. They were all envious of a man who could do this. They believed he was brilliant for keeping the theme from them all the while and for having spent such laborious time in preparation for this awesome manuscript.

Forty-five minutes of this tingling dialogue was about all anyone could take. The audience was drained and so was the speaker. When he felt in his stomach he had taken them to the border of reason, he started to wind up. He orated, "I'm not going to tell you what the word is. Some of you may know but no one has correctly said it. But each of you will see it as a vision written right in front of your eyes as you leave this hall.

You will see it emblazoned on the doors as you exit." With this he moved from the podium and to the thunderous applause he justly deserved, he strode to his seat.

There were a few more remarks by other speakers, but the audience was edgy and could hardly wait to leave their seats so they could see the apparition at the doorway. The president made the final good-bye and dismissed the class. They threw their caps in the air and, almost without congratulating each other, sped to the doors to receive "the word."

And there it was in the same block, black letters the professor had seen upon entering the auditorium. But from this way, exiting the hall rather than coming in, the word was "PULL."

A small error, but he wasn't entirely wrong. In the world of business, influence means an awful lot. There is the old saying, "It's not what you know but who you know." I'm not speaking here of the situation of the child who preys on his parent's good name or connections. I am speaking of the realm of prospecting through referrals. That is "pull" in the best possible sense. The odds are being swayed in your favor when you approach a prospect in a more favorable, warm mode rather than a cold call basis. We are taught from earliest contact to qualify our leads by finding out as much information as we can about them. A proper introduction ranks highest on the list of qualifications of new people. It is tougher for a contact to refuse an interview when the introduction is being made by mentioning the name of a respected friend or business associate. There is an aura of respect for the other person's business judgement, as well as a sense of curiosity about what the other person is doing about his or her finances. Of all the methods of prospecting, using referrals is the most sensible and, at the same time, the easiest.

Consider your own reaction if you were approached on the telephone by someone who wanted to talk with you about computer equipment. The person started with the line, "I'm calling to arrange a time when we might meet and discuss a computer system which has proven to be interesting and valuable to many insurance salespeople."

Now consider that your best friend's name was Burt Meisel and the phone call came this way: "I recently had a meeting with Burt Meisel. I'm calling to arrange a time when we might meet and discuss a computer system which has proven to be interesting and valuable to many insurance salespeople." Think about it carefully and give the above two approaches a fair test in your mind.

With the first, your sense of sales resistance probably stirred and your mind was in gear to try not to hear the whole story before you got your chance to object. You were recalling all the thoughts you had regarding computers such as you already had one, or you can't afford one at this time, or your company is going to come out with a specialized system just for its agents, or other ideas which got you in the computer objecting mode.

With the second approach your thoughts are more on the facts of what your friend was doing regarding computers and how your plans fit in with his. You think about his business operation and your own and where there may be areas of research for improved productivity. The onus is taken away from buying computer services and why you should consider the same or new services which your friend is considering. Look back and see that the approach did not even say what Burt Meisel had done about computers; it only said there had been a recent meeting.

All the senses of resistance were down and the sense of curiosity was up. This is not to say using someone else's name as an entree will guarantee an interview every time you use it. It only changes the numbers game in your favor so that fewer of the prospects are "out or busy." And that is the purpose of successful selling: to reduce the incidents of failure and increase the chances for victory. The purpose of any competition is to win. In selling the purpose of any sales interview is to sell. Therefore, any positive type of conditioning or preparation is an adjunct to a successful interview.

Yet what about the times when you are not successful? The opposite of success is failure. Have you failed when you do not succeed? I don't think so. How is it possible not to succeed and yet, at the same time, not be a failure? Is this merely a play on words? No, it is only a revelation of what the career really entails. Since it is an impossibility to sell all of the cases we present, each of us will develop an average sales to interviews ratio.

I have always felt the ladies hosiery industry was an interesting phenomenon. We men never fully understand the impact of the words, "I just ran my hose." In my house, I always heard that a lot with a wife and four daughters. It seemed it always came at the most unexpected time which appeared to be quite often. Therefore, I wonder if there is an air of planned obsolescence which goes into the manufacturing of ladies hosiery. In the planning sessions for inventory control and sales the hosiery makers must plot both the endurance and fault factors for their material. In that respect they are no different than our business or any other business. There is a certain profitable percentage and a certain cost percentage. I hear commercials on TV which shout "run-proof hose" or show someone trying to put a nail through a stocking without results. If that is true, there is the possibility of making lasting stockings instead of those that run on the first wearing or even on the first fitting. But the business goes on and each lady hopes she gets a reasonable amount of wear out of each pair.

No matter if it is stockings, autos, speeches, or insurance, no industry or profession is without so-called "failure." The only thing I can think of which is automatic and appears to be infallible is the growth of government. There is no way to stop that. So, if we have to have some "no's" in order to get the "yes's" why do we have so much fear and reaction to rejection? The answer has to come in the human feelings which all of us have. Some of us can analyze statistics better than others and handle the results better than others. We should not have any feelings of animosity toward any prospect who rejects us; keep in mind, it was we who called them and not the opposite. We asked them to take action and they had choices. In spite of all the logic we can show, sometimes they say thumbs up and sometimes thumbs down.

As I said earlier, disappointment was understandable but discouragement was not. This, too, depends upon the human equation. Each of us is built differently and we will handle our business relations in different fashions. I believe it is the job of the managerial corps to better prepare young agents so they are not shattered by the experiences which are an everyday occurrence in our business. Too frequently, the emphasis is put on the success ratio and little discussion given to the miss ratio. It is then understandable for the rookie agent to be surprised and have difficulty understanding why they are being rejected. It was never explained to them properly and not even handled properly.

More often than we like to think, the rejection should come earlier and more dramatically in the career of a young agent. In more cases than is happening now, the rejection should come at the time the career is examined. The supervisory corps should be more honest with novices and tell them early this is not the profession for them. Many of our unsuccessful agents are merely a mirrored reflection of the inabilities of their managers. More people should be turned down from signing life insurance selling contracts. It would be best for the industry, both the buying side and the selling side. If the candidate obviously does not have the attributes to make progress he or she should be advised not to enter. It would be the kindest rejection of all and might not even be considered as rejection but only the dead bones truth.

The rejection comes, however, and we have to live with it. The real question is how do we handle it. I had a firsthand opportunity to observe the matter being handled by members of my own family. We were at a brunch at a restaurant prior to going to a football game. My wife, Sharon, and daughters Bonnie, Shelley, and Dori were there. Sharon is fully familiar with the selling highs and lows having lived twenty-eight years of it with me, along with handling the operation of our company, I.B. Meisel Presentations. Although as close as a spouse can be in all matters, I think the wavering cycles and true emotions can only be felt by those doing the asking and getting the good or bad answers.

Bonnie is a produce broker for international companies and understands the vagaries of selling although, we must admit, ours are different than any other industry. Dori is a senior at Michigan State University studying telecommunications. Her understanding of the selling attitudes are limited to those she has learned at home, being in a selling family, and from part-time jobs she has had which relate to the public. Dori is considering entering the life insurance business when she graduates so her interest in this subject in intense. Shelley is in the life insurance business so she is dodging the slings and arrows just like the rest of us.

It was December and the selling for the record books was all wrapped-up. We were having a stimulating conversation due to the fact Shelley had a very fine year and also qualified for the Million Dollar Round Table in her first year. Dori asked Shelley, "Does the rejection really bother you?" I know we would all have our own philosophical answers and I have given you many of mine in this book, but now I was very interested in the answer Shelley would give on this, the first anniversary of her entering the business. I felt it would be a pure answer and I listened intently. She said, "Most of the time it doesn't bother me because I was ready for it since Dad told me each interview was part of a sale. If it is someone I don't know well, it doesn't bother me at all but if it is a relative or someone for whom I have special feelings and really care, it does bother me."

"When a close relative gives me a hard time or gives me silly objections, it does bother me. But. . .you can't take it personally."

I don't believe it is possible to have a finer answer than that. *"You can't take it personally."* The client is not objecting to you or even your product; they are objecting to the factors in their lives which make them say the things they say about a product which can't do anything but help them.

Therefore, as we go out making our appointed rounds and we endure and enjoy all the elements which go into a fruitful life insurance selling venture, and it seems like the whole world is out or busy, don't take it personally.

12

Getting Out or Getting Busy

Sometimes for our own sanity and productivity we had better make ourselves be out or busy. A car can not be run continuously without periods of rest and maintenance. No machine goes on forever without requiring some downtime for rejuvination. Neither can we, as salespeople, perpetually be in motion. We have to have downtime in order to be ready for the uptime.

Due to the nature of our business we are the other end of the equation as much as we are the ones to hear the "outs" and the "busys." We run active careers seeing great numbers of people in order to complete our ultimate goals. The very nature of our profession keeps us away from our offices frequently and keeps us on the phone when we are in the office. We have to be out in order to meet and present our interviews to our clientele. When we're in the office, we had better be using the phone for our new prospecting and our necessary and ongoing service work.

Our industry does an excellent job of presenting us with a fair expose of the potential problems of "all work and no play." The Million Dollar Round Table presents sessions on "The Whole Person" concept and the effects of stress as a regular and ongoing part of the continuing education program. Our national and local magazines and bulletins constantly present articles by famous lecturers and writers on the subject of stress management and the keeping of our lives in balance. They're right; it is necessary to keep a regulated check on our activities.

Most of us in this business are aggressive, hyper competitors. We have to be in a business where we must be totally self-starting. The jealous stories about those individuals who have fabulous production records, only because their parents were wealthy, or they had a background in some other high visibility field such as sports, are true for only a handful of people in our endeavor. Almost everyone is doing exactly the same thing, finding and qualifying good potential clients. In order to do all the details which are necessary to fulfill our desires, we engage in a tremendous amount of education, service work, and many other methods of public relation, client building activities.

Our time is made-up of schedules, appointments, deadlines, and points of no return. We live in an atmosphere of pressure. Our companies, peers, and living standards force us to strive ever more. The first purpose of any occupation is to make a living. Then comes the stated altruistic purpose of providing for the public whatever good or service we offer. We put ourselves under tremendous strains and pressures. Like a client of mine once said after returning from an examiner's office for a stress test, "Burt, that was simple. That was no test of stress. I went there prepared for it. If the insurance company wants to see some real stress, they should have sent the doctor to examine me while I'm working in my plant." As an aside, he got his insurance rated standard but he did say an awful lot in that little quip about the exam he had to take.

It was his impression that leaving his office to appear elsewhere under a controlled situation to measure stress was no indication of the normal, daily pressure cooker in which he labors in his own job. Actually, showing up in a doctor's office for a physical, along with the other scheduled events of a business day, is not my idea of relief. Yet, for his little exaggerated quip on why he even needed that test, the culprit is the way we handle our working lives and not the outside activities.

Because we are competitive and because we are aggressive, we get involved in time grabbing of the tightest nature. We listen to study tapes while we dress in the morning. We have them in our cars. We do appointments over meals. We attempt to be polyphasic in everything we do. We always want to make one minute be worth more than it is. We forbid ourselves to have an unstructured moment. And we don't say "no." We are macho men and women and, if someone asks us to head up a committee or project, we feel they must know more about our schedules, capabilities, and limitations than we do. Besides, we convince ourselves it is good public relations.

We love contests and campaigns. If our companies aren't having one then the agency is. If the agency isn't, we try to make up one of our own to stimulate our production further than it has ever gone before. We all want to be the first insurance agent to walk on the moon. It probably won't do any good. We'll most likely find that one of the great, big department stores beat us there, complete with an insurance and financial planning counter with the latest in "do-it-yourself, hands on" computer data inputting.

When the jealousy gremlin creeps in urging us to beat our neighbor or associate we further strain ourselves. If the other guy can write a quillion dollar policy, we feel we can write a trikillion dollar policy. The companies or agencies operating outside "The Fifteen Percent Syndrome" ask us, on special occasions, to do something extra for a short-term cause. We want to be a part of all the success syndromes, all the company clubs, all the industry clubs, and still more. We always want more and we want it right away. But instant success is like instant coffee; it still takes time to boil the water.

Outside of the industry, we also drive ourselves to further competition. We engage in sports, charities, civic affairs, our children's affairs, and some in various nefarious affairs with the same "fast lane" zeal. We need these outside things but not for more stress. That's a problem, being on the go all the time. We are lectured about the fact we are type A; at least it seems there are more A's than B's. We are also told there is more than one kind of stress and we can't be without it completely. The trick is how to control it. This gives rise to the notion that we must make ourselves unavailable sometimes in order to regroup. I don't mean to be unavailable for one chore because we are handling another. I mean the deliberate and utter avoidance of the work scene in favor of the relaxing side of life.

The body is the most fabulous machine in the world but it must be kept in balance. Stress in doses is OK. Relaxation in proportion is important. Even a slice of laziness doesn't hurt once in a while. I believe each person should have that one little Eden of his or her own, which is complete and blissful oblivion from the normalcy of our routines. For some this is the theater or going out to dinner. For others, it is charity or civic work. Others get vigorously involved in sports. I have noticed at MDRT meetings a great proportion of us who do the most running during the year in order to qualify, also do the pavement pounding every morning. This is good. It is a form of vacating the brain while the mind is put on auto pilot for the duration of the jog.

Some meditate. Some read novels which is a tremendous mode of turn-off. It seems as if one gets involved totally in a good book all other hindrances disappear from the brain. That is the object: to let the batteries recharge themselves in nature's way. All parents should be able to relax with their children in spite of the fact it seems they are stress carriers and not receivers. In our business, or in any other, there is no way to earn well above the average income by working nine to five. I hear a lot of agents telling me how few hours they really work. I listen but I don't hear them. Maybe they are on the scene less than some of their counterparts but I submit all systems are tuned to the work frequency more time than they wish to admit.

Since we are on call so much of the time, either directly on the producing front or with all the fringe areas to which we must give precious time, it is vital that all the time we spend with our spouses and our children be quality time. When you're with them be with them. There is nothing more important you have to do. Time flies. At first we measure our working career in decades. Then it is years; then months. This also reflects the time we have with the ones we love. Don't count the time; make the time count.

Travel is a beautiful change. Not only do you remove the body from the hectic workbench but, in about a day or two, the brain will follow. Then, when you have all the parts together in a spot away from the phone, the staff, and the clientele, you can really start to rejuvenate. Sharon and I are fortunate in the fact we are able to travel as much as we do for the public speaking part of our business. We go to some of the most beautiful spots in the world. Sometimes I am doing a full day's seminar or, on others, I am only working one hour. We are treated royally on these speeches. However, no matter if it is one hour or a full day of lecturing, I am on the spot for a commitment of time. I have deadlines and I have to perform accordingly. Travel is one of our forms of stress reduction so, in addition to this heavy schedule, we arrange one trip which is completely for us with all the efforts going on relax circuitry.

I will go into a little detail about how we plan a trip so we are really turned off from the world. About ten years ago, I made a speech in London, Ontario, at the Holiday Inn City Centre. The speech was booked about a year before the date and when I heard Holiday Inn, I pictured the green and yellow buildings which I had seen for many years. My brother and sister-in-law, Chuck and Gail, went with us on this trip since we were going to drive on to Toronto for the weekend.

When we arrived, it was clear to see this was more like a Las Vegas hotel than a roadside hostelry. It was about twenty-two stories with a marble floor in the lobby, bellmen, fine restaurants, a mall attached, and fabulous

Canadian service. We had a gorgeous suite with a large parlor and really enjoyed the couple of days we spent there.

One day in December of that same year I leaned back in my chair, exhausted to the bone from year-end business activity. I was talking with Sharon on the phone and I even had my eyes closed. I told her how tired I was and how I wished we could get away for a couple of days because that was all the time I had. I also said we should go somewhere which didn't entail too much travel time. She suggested this beautiful hotel in which we truly felt completely relaxed and which was only a two hour drive from Detroit. We didn't have to crimp ourselves packing since it was a motor trip, so the relaxing started with the packing. Chuck and Gail were able to join us and we have now made the return to Mecca ten years in a row.

In order to cope with all the things our business takes and still remain on the upbeat side, all of us must have a time and a place when we are completely turned off and our client who is calling says to himself, "Darn it, my agent is out or busy."

Even though we enjoy the Holiday Inn City Centre so much, I am sure there are bigger and gaudier hotels to visit. So what is the big attraction? The answer is the attitude of the people. From the moment we check in with the concierges Victoria Viner and Mary Lynn Scott, we are in orbit once again. Two very pretty ladies but also two beautiful personalities and attitudes. They have our names on the list and they pronounce it correctly. We feel welcome immediately and, once again, realize the business meters are broken. There is no hassle checking in and if there were, we would forgive it just because of the greeting we get.

Inn keeper Mike Whittaker is a proper gentleman of the Barbados mold. We know why his staff is so pleasant; his enthusiasm and interest in our well-being radiate. We feel important but we also do not feel it is an attitude not given to all the other guests. We have met Mike's wife, Denise, and gone to dinner with them. We feel like friends and not patrons.

This last section was not a commercial for a hotel but it was a commercial for total relaxation. It just so happens this hotel in this city fulfills everything for us when we want to be "out or busy."

So, when you work, work. When you play, play. The public will always be there, including that portion which will be "out or busy."

We now have this trip down to a science of no decisions, no stress, no deadlines, and no hint of pressure. Our biggest decision of each day is to find a nice place to eat. And believe me, we've found them. In fact, we now have a ritual of attending the same one on the last Sunday night we are there. We have become friends with the owner and we feel completely at home. We never take ties and if there is a dress code in any restaurant, we just don't go there. One Super Bowl Sunday, we didn't even get dressed until eight o'clock that evening to go to dinner.

The after Christmas sales are on so we get 20% to 50% off on purchases. Fortunately, for our side of the border, the U.S. dollar is temporarily worth about thirty-one percent more than the Canadian, so the shopping is a bargain frenzy.

Everything considered, this trip is all we could want for relaxing purposes. People ask us, "What do you do in London, Ontario, in the middle of winter? There is nothing there." We say, "That is why we go." But there is something there which makes this trip an obligation each year rather than just a vacation; an obligation, but a labor of love. That one thing is something we should adapt readily and openly into our businesses: willing service.